# ASHTAVAKRA GITA

A dialogue between
RESOURCEFULNESS & WISDOM

a translation of the ancient Sanskrit text

Ashwini Kumar Aggarwal

जय गुरुदेव

© 2022, Author
ISBN13: 978-93-92201-86-8  Paperback Edition
ISBN13: 978-93-92201-98-1  Hardbound Edition
ISBN13: 978-93-92201-31-8  Digital Edition

This work is licensed under a Creative Commons Attribution 4.0 International License. Please visit
https://creativecommons.org/licenses/by/4.0/

Title: **Ashtavakra Gita**
SubTitle: **A dialogue between Resourcefulness & Wisdom**
Author: **Ashwini Kumar Aggarwal**

Printed and Published by
**Devotees of Sri Sri Ravi Shankar Ashram**
34 Sunny Enclave, Devigarh Road,
Patiala 147001, Punjab, India

https://advaita56.weebly.com/
The Art of Living Centre

https://www.artofliving.org/

13th May 2022, Beloved Gurudev's Birthday, Mohini Ekadashi Parashurama Dvadashi, Pradosh Vrat, Shukla Paksha
On this day in 1967 Zakir Husain elected President, 1952 Jawaharlal Nehru becomes Prime Minister, 1916 Native American Indian Day 1st observance, 1884 Institute of Electrical & Electronics Engineers setup, 1767 Mozart's first opera at age 11 premiers.
Vikram Samvat 2079 Rakshasa, Saka Era 1944 Shubhakrit

1st Edition May 2022

जय गुरुदेव

# Dedication

## Sri Sri Ravi Shankar

> Wisdom & Resourcefulness giver

Specially dedicated to: My mother KAVITA

Who only last month in April 2022 enquired happily: So what are you writing now? I responded – ASHTAVAKRA. She beamed– O Ashtavakra Gita – May the Lord be with You.

# Blessing

YOU ARE FREE RIGHT NOW

You are total. You are full. You have all that you need. Do not underestimate yourself. A Guru is there to show you what you are.

Sri Sri Ravi Shankar<br>Discourse on Ashtavakra Gita, Bangalore Ashram, Devi Hall<br>1991

# Acknowledgements

Lord's Patiala visit on 3rd April 2022 during Chaitra Navratri infuses Brahman Consciousness in us all.

# Table of Contents

BLESSING .................................................................................. 4

PREFACE ................................................................................... 6

PRAYER ..................................................................................... 7

INTRODUCTION ........................................................................ 8

CAST OF CHARACTERS ........................................................... 10

    *Qualifications Prerequisites* .............................................. 14

SECTION 1 THE BASIC QUESTION ......................................... 15

SECTION 2 THE ANSWER REALIZED ...................................... 27

SECTION 3A ANSWER EXAMINED FOR RAW ........................ 41

SECTION 3B ANSWER PONDERED FOR A YOGI .................... 45

SECTION 4 THE ANSWER PRAISED ....................................... 49

SECTION 5 THE ANSWER SIMPLIFIED ................................... 53

SECTION 6 QUEST FOR THE GENUINE ................................. 57

SECTION 7 THE GENUINE IS NEAR AT HAND ....................... 61

SECTION 8 WHAT TO AVOID .................................................. 65

SECTION 9 LET GO WELL IN TIME ......................................... 69

SECTION 10 MOHA INFATUATION LUST .............................. 73

SECTION 11 DISSOCIATION ................................................... 77

SECTION 12 SON TO SUN ....................................................... 81

SECTION 13 SATIATED GIRLFRIEND ..................................... 85

SECTION 14 PEACE SOLIDIFIES ............................................. 89

SECTION 15 BE BOLD YET NATURAL .................................... 91

LATIN TRANSLITERATION CHART ........................................ 101

SANSKRIT VERSES FOR CHANTING ..................................... 102

SANSKRIT GRAMMAR ............................................................ 137

CONJUGATION PROCESS OF VERB ..................................... 140

DECLENSION PROCESS OF NOUN ....................................... 142

REFERENCES ............................................................................. 143
EPILOGUE ................................................................................ 144

# Preface

During a trek to virgin nature, the mind stops chattering. Unbelievable things happen to the consciousness.

The body doesn't complain.
The heart feels nice and warm.
And the Lord walks in.

I first heard about Ashtavakra Gita in 1999 at Swadesh Vig's home in Model Town, Delhi. I had come for Guruji's darshan with a long letter to clear my head of the maze of thoughts. I got the audience with the Lord courtesy of Sukhi bhaiya. Guruji was sitting on his bed in the bedroom, Nityanand Trehan was sitting on the floor. Sri Sri glanced thru the letter slowly, then after a moment of contemplation said calmly – "Hear the Ashtavakra Gita". I asked – "What is that Guruji"? Nityanand replied – "You can get a set of 33 cassettes from the Ashram Divine Shop, and you must hear one discourse a day". Then Guruji added – "You do TTC and become a Teacher".

# Prayer

शान्तिपाठः
ॐ स॒ह ना॑ववतु । स॒ह नौ॑ भुनक्तु । स॒ह वी॒र्यं॑ करवावहै ।
ते॒ज॒स्वि ना॒वधी॑तमस्तु मा वि॑द्विषा॒वहै᳚ ॥
ॐ शान्तिः॒ शान्तिः॒ शान्तिः॑ ॥

oṃ saha nāvavatu | saha nau bhunaktu | saha vīryaṃ karavāvahai | tejasvi nāvadhītamastu mā vidviṣāvahai ||
oṃ śānti śānti śāntiḥ ||

## Peace Invocation
O Pure Loving Grace!
May we be taken care of along with our family and friends.
May we enjoy socializing and eating together.
May we support each other's vision and growth.
May our intellect be open to new ideas and changing trends.
May we spend more time in praise than abuse, may we talk of each other's virtues rather than harp on vices.

Peace in our heart, in our body and in our environs.

# Introduction

The Energy signifying WEALTH, SKILL and RESOURCEFULNESS manifested in the body of the King of Mithila, named Janaka, father of Sita of Ramayana fame.

Since Janaka had everything, his thoughts turned more and more towards Vairagya, the dispassion force essential for union with Brahman the Absolute.

*In Indian tradition, it is said, the Lord seeks out his beloved devotee, and engineers an event that culminates in enlightenment.*

King Janaka once in his Royal Palace, happened to doze off in the midst of a lengthy day to day facts reporting by his administration and secretaries.

In the midst of a short slumber, he dreamt that he was extremely hungry, stumbling along alone in an endless expanse. Unable to contain his ravenous hunger, he prayed desperately for a morsel of food, and per chance spied a piece of dried roti (that is customarily) put out for the birds. Immediately he picked it up, and was about to sit in a shady spot to munch it.

At that instant a huge bird swooped from the skies, grabbed the roti from his hands and was gone instantly. This shattered his nerve; he cried out bitterly.

That broke his reverie, and he found himself comfortably ensconced on his Royal Throne in his Grand Palace.

Back to his senses and fully alert, King Janaka enquired of his assembly:

WHAT IS TRUTH?

Was the slumber Truth, was the dream Truth, was the emotion of extreme hunger Truth, was the helplessness at the bird's snatch Truth?

Was the cry of desperation Truth?
Is this Royal Assembly the Truth?

Is Palace with well-oiled machinery Truth?
Are the Ministers and Secretaries Truth?

Is Hunger and Poverty Truth,
Is Comfort and Happiness Truth?

No one could satisfy his quest. Until ASHTAVAKRA the embodiment of Brahman, the energy signifying WISDOM walked in.

## Cast of Characters

King Janaka represents Resourcefulness.
- He is young and fit i.e., a body that can go the extra mile and bring home the bounty, come what may.
- His mind is alert and flexible, he engineers solutions to unravel knotty situations, he is bright enough to circumvent danger, and come up with smart ideas to make living a success.
- He is large hearted, so fears do not stick, emotions do not become stormy, his ready acceptance and humility make lasting friends and networks.

Ashtavakra represents Wisdom.
- He is old, far older than the denizens of the entire village, with a wealth of experience of myriad situations and tricky persons, having been through all that nature could *season*, or that man could *excite*.
- Ashtavakra is solidified peace; he is sculpted in bliss.

What happens when Resourcefulness meets Wisdom?

This is the story...
>    of their timeless talk,
>    a languid conversation,
>    a meaningful dialogue
that establishes peace, faith, bliss and longevity.

Do not think that **Resourcefulness** and **Wisdom** are alien to you. The energy that runs through **Janaka** and **Ashtavakra** is awake and alive within you, it just needs <u>some attention, some quality time, some purposeful silent reflection, some spiritual practices as ordained by your Guru</u>.

On a personal level, Janaka is the country's King. He is the father of Sita, the maiden representing planet earth, *Bhu-Devi*. Sita is not yet born at the time of the dialogue, later on she goes on to become the consort of Lord Rama, the rapture that we all seek, the Divine presence.

So the dialogue that occurs is instrumental in giving birth to Sita. She is the purity that attracts the Divine and unites it with planet earth.

Ashtavakra (ashta-vakra) is the eight vectored-forcefield. (*We notice the usage of the word "vakra" in the verses that praise Ganesha, viz. vakra-tund mahakaya = Lord that defies the linear forces of logic*). He represents command over the four cardinal directions (North East South West) and the four intermediate directions (NE SE SW NW). Eight is also symbolic of infinity ($\infty$ vs 8). Ashtavakra simply means the eight energies that need to be harnessed and attended to. <u>The eight forces needed to bring total balance in life, in work, in play, in entertainment and the beyond.</u>

Happiness[1N] Love[2NE] Light[3E] Kindness[4SE] Gratefulness[5S] Humility[6SW] Surrender[7W] Sincerity[8NW].

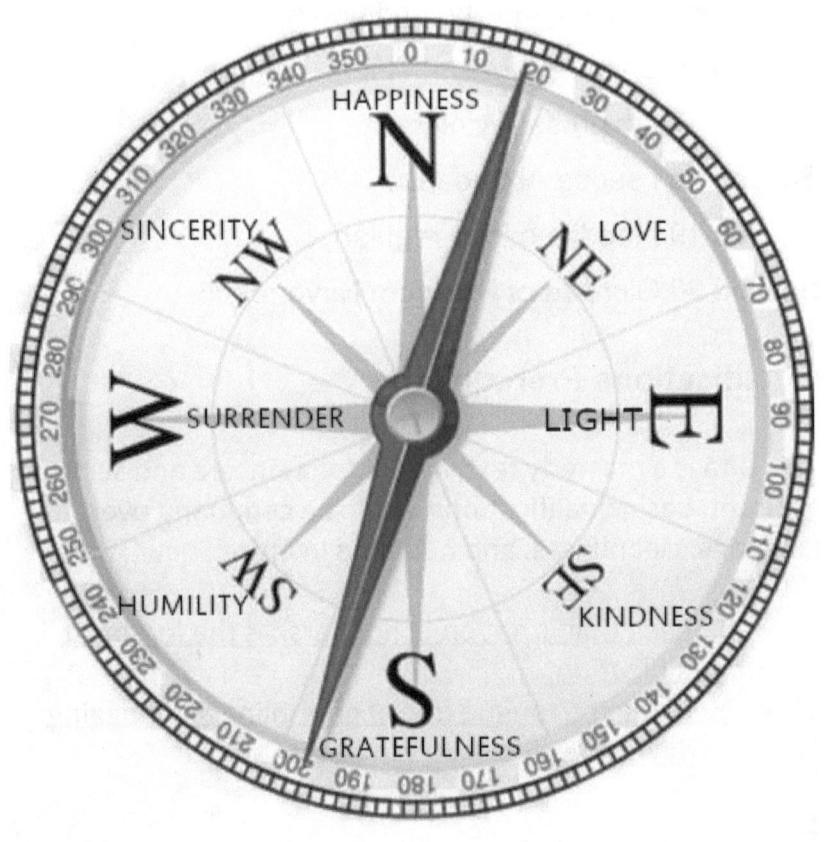

Refer verse 1.2 क्षमा आर्जव दया तोष सत्यम् ।

- क्षमा = Forgiveness = Humility[6SW] + Surrender[7W]
- आर्जव = Earnestness = Sincerity[7NW]
- दया = Compassion = Kindness[4SE]
- तोष = Contentment = Happiness[1N]+Gratefulness[5S]
- सत्यम् = Truth = Light[3E] + Love[2NE]

There are 298 verses arranged under 20 topics.

(following sections shall be updated soon...
Section 16 Divine is always Mine
Section 17 I express Divinity
Section 18 I sense Abundance
Section 19 I Meditate long regularly
Section 20 Glimpse of Freedom Nirvana)

## Qualifications Prerequisites

This Gita is a masterly text, meant for a sincere and serious aspirant. Basic qualifications include a command over language, cleanliness, and neatness in attire.

- <u>Speech that is not cruel nor harsh is the foremost qualification.</u>
- <u>Keeping the tongue free of grumbling and nagging in day-to-day life is very important</u>

Other essential qualifications so that knowledge gets imbibed are:
- Respectfulness
- Readiness to serve with cheerfulness
- Maintain discipline for a year with frugal lifestyle
- Truthfulness and candor in communication
- Regularly walking the path ordained by one's Master

# Section 1 The Basic Question

**1.1** Resourcefulness sits at the feet of Wisdom. With a cheerful countenance he asks - my beloved master - how may i deepen my experience of life? How may i become free to explore more? Lastly how may i resolve within afterwards?

∞∞∞

**1.2** Wisdom instantly replies - O humble son - if thee desire freedom, then shun the sensual distractions forthwith. Avoid the mundane, do not engage with people in arbitrary talk, restrict your pleasure yearnings.

If thee desire to expand your horizon, then practice the virtues  forgiveness-earnestness-kindness-gratefulness-truthfulness.

1.3 Lessen your identification with and dependence on the external objects, whether hankering for big plots, large amounts of water for day-to-day activity, various electromechanical gadgets and machines, perfumes and cosmetics, undue storage that consumes unnecessary space.

What shall aid your freedom to move about and explore and experience; is knowing that there is a divine spark inside you, that divinity is part of your being.

∞∞∞

1.4 Once you can lessen your dependence on men and machinery, you shall immediately feel joyful, peaceful, and freed.

1.5 Time and again erase your labels of husband or boss, engineer or doctor, or other social and fame related attachments. These are simply draped over you like coat over skin that needs to be discarded during a shower or sleep. See that you are bigger than these labels, and feel the freedom instantly.

∞∞∞

1.6 Work and Entertainment, salary and expenses, are a cyclical occurrence, so why give them undue importance? Know that you are capable of these, and in such knowledge find rest.

1.7 The one divine that cares for you is free isn't he? Realize his closeness and instantly experience freedom.

∞∞∞

1.8 An inflated ego becomes brittle and self-injurious, relax your hold on family and work, and experience the joy.

1.9 Strengthen your faith and temper your virtues in the fire of self-enquiry. Let go of limited identity and superfluous skill, the letting go diminishes lack and craving, and makes one happy.

∞∞∞

1.10 As long as the mind hankers after family and work, the hold of ego becomes stubborn. Remember time and again to let go of work and family, allow your consciousness to expand beyond and joy filters in.

1.11 Reality is not physical, it is notional; remember to tell yourself time and again - All is Well, I am a King, I am free. Soon the thoughts you nourish become a physical reality - this is a universal truth.

∞∞∞

1.12 The Soul is a witness; it is connected to the Lord and is hence all-pervading and complete. The Soul is ever free, ever aware, ever effortless, unattached, non-oscillating and tranquil. However, by the cover of family and work it becomes clouded and doubtful and forgetful.

1.13 Diminish the hold of work and family to allow the Soul to Shine through. Meditate on the stillness within, Meditate on the inner silence, and realize you are firm and uncompromised.

∞∞∞

1.14 My dear son - disentangle again and again from society, people, possessions. With determination connect again and again with the Self, and allow happiness to spring.

1.15 Allow the faith to strengthen that the Soul doesn't need entanglements, nor does it need over work. The Soul is all awareness without blemish. So during Meditation do not rake up the thoughts of family and work, allow the Meditation to happen with an attitude of - i am nobody - i don't need to put effort - i do not need any wish to be fulfilled at this time.

∞∞∞

1.16 I pervade this whole creation, i permeate all matter, the one underlying purity connects us all, may my mind not entertain any base thoughts.

1.17 I remain untouched and unaffected by my circumstances and situations; my soul is the abode of calmness. My intellect is not narrow, my heart is fearless, may i aim for the highest.

∞∞∞

1.18 Accept and appreciate both the physical form and the chemical biochemistry, only then can family or work friction be prevented.

**1.19** The big screen is always there, whether or not a movie is projected, it remains. So also, the supreme consciousness pervades a body inside, and irrespective of the presence of anybody it is all outside as well.

∞∞∞

**1.20** Just as all atoms are filled with space, so does Divinity fill all men

Janaka or Resourcefulness hears the teaching of
Wisdom intensely,

each word and sentence
    making deep impressions in his brain, and
    clearing away any residual doubt or cloud.

After a moment of deep silence, Janaka bursts forth.

**Section 2 The Answer Realized**

# I AM PURE. I AM WHOLE.
O Lord! Gratefulness for this realization.

**2.1** Aho! Niranjana. I am untouched and unalloyed. Nature and Man have not dented my intrinsic purity or peace one bit.

All this time i had just gone into a spin that was wholly imagined.

ӨӨӨ

**2.2** Just as my body attains importance due to my mind's presence, so does the Universe attain importance due to my body-mind complex.

Hence my universe is very personal and unique, none's universe is the same as mine.

**2.3** When this fact becomes crystal clear that my situation is entirely different from his and hers, easily i step into his shoes and experience his world, and easily my world gets detached from me and fades away.

What gets detached are my botherations, thanks to the viewpoint shown to me by my Master.

ϴϴϴ

**2.4** I now see that the waves and storms and whirlpools are but all tiny bubbles dotting the mighty ocean.

Each such wave is a complete universe to its individual atoms, so are all these men carrying varying notions and imaginations of the one same universe that is nothing but the Lord.

**2.5** Just as any fabric is the white cotton thread, so is this creation just the pure unalloyed divinity.

ⴲⴲⴲ

**2.6** Just as sweet is the taste of each sip of sugarcane juice, so is this divine sweetness that is within me the one thing outside of me in other men too.

**2.7** Just as imagination of various men pronounces different judgements on each's predicament, so is the same situation interpreted differently by each one of us.

Pure imagination is the cause of each one's fearsome universe, a Saint sees the purity alone sans imagination.

ΘΘΘ

**2.8** Wisdom is my very nature, i am naught but awareness.

My imagination is the cause of the universe, and my thoughts and attitude the universe reflects back to me in name and form.

**2.9** Oh! Yes, the fearsome creation is the concoction of my sensuous broodings in weakened moments.

ΘΘΘ

**2.10** Eureka, i see a mud pot breaking to become earth, a torrent of water disappearing into the ocean, feverish passion getting diluted over time.

So with foresight i can reduce and prevent my fearsome moments, and no longer shall i experience hell.

**2.11** Salutations to this wonderful divinity inside me, O what purity and strength i have within.

With awareness i can eclipse any thorny situation and all bitter persons to make my life heavenly, sweet and meaningful.

ΘΘΘ

**2.12** Goodness Me! Look at this superhuman being that is me!

As far as i see, it is my body alone, all are in me. I reach to all corners of creation; all corners meet in me.

**2.13** O what a prodigy the Lord created! His perfect creation i am!

I feel so alive and brilliant. I feel so solid and eternally youthful.

ɵɵɵ

**2.14** O ain't i a miracle! I am in utter awe of myself.

I command all thee yonder, none brook my command, i own it all, yet naught goes to my head.

**2.15** Knowledge-Process of Knowing-Knower this threesome is the entire phenomenon.

When i am objective and calm, no situation is troublesome, no person is bothersome.

ɵɵɵ

**2.16** Unbelongingness and unacceptance of others, rewarding my family not on merit but on relationships, and shying away from acknowledging the better man and not helping him because i am spending all on my family due to infatuation, this is how misery begins in life, this is how i open the gates of hell for myself.

If only someone can peel away the skin of moha from my eyes, if someone could point out my blunder of sinking my fortune for my untruthful relations who would never help me later...

may i be duly warned of bad company and heed the warning...

may i understand that enemies are always within and never without...

I hope i rise above my relative ego and attain the ultimate purity.

**2.17** Even though i was born pure, yet due to impure siblings and relatives i experienced hell.

Not because they were impure, but because i couldn't prevent myself from associating with them and helping them.

Unknowingly i divided my wealth amongst them and became a pauper.

Someday someone shall point it out to me and by moving out of the circle of inferior family members, i shall regain my purity and wealth.

Many times my family members are not bad, but they are undeserving due to ignorance and undisciplined lifestyle, yet i wish for them to prosper and go out of the way to help them. This becomes my downfall; infatuation is a hidden illness that strikes down even the great.

I pray that i use discrimination in my relations and steer clear of the unwise if i wish to achieve my goals.

ӨӨӨ

**2.18** When i steer clear of infatuation, i realize there is no bondage, i am free.

I am free to attain success since i have dropped the illusionary relatives.

The drama created by my siblings no longer rules my emotions, my trajectory moves away from pitfalls towards sure success.

I recognize that family members cannot always be right, i understand that even though they are my family yet my aims are different from theirs, and the twain shall never meet.

I get enlightened that people who are not related to me can be my biggest asset, since their thoughts match mine, moreover they know that i am not trapped by infatuation towards them.

ɵɵɵ

**2.19** O Yes! I just realized this and became free of infatuation. O Yes! Having discarded the impure bodies i am now one with the ultimate purity.

No longer can my emotions rule me, no longer can my intellect be clouded.

**2.20** O Wow! My Body, Your Body, His Body, Her Body. This is the entire gamut of Heaven and Hell. Sometimes this body is hell and that body Heaven, or vice versa. Sometimes more are Heavenly, very little Hellish; and vice versa.

O Fear! Now i can see through You. Fear! You are naught other than my clouded reasoning. Prison and Suffering! You BOTH are just a small portion of my life that helps me develop some appropriate emotion. O Well, so be it.

ΘΘΘ

**2.21** O Wow! These bodies have fused and melted and become one. These emotions have become diluted and effervescent. The foliage is all me, the city is all me in myriad forms reflecting myself. I revel in this expanded consciousness. i feel so unattached to fear or suffering. O i am untouched by lack or misery.

**2.22** I feel a oneness with the world that transcends my body consciousness. i feel i am the energy that moves in all and expresses all. Earlier i had limited myself to a small frame, that had caged my emotions, imagination and reason.

ooo

**2.23** i see now that i am the ocean yonder with might storms and frolicking waves, with still waters that run deep, with maze of pockets teeming with life, full of racing thoughts.

**2.24** and when my consciousness expands to include the creation, my thoughts become very thin as the spent storms due to the dropping of the winds.

The fear within finds no person to trouble, the pain no longer has any victim.

ΘΘΘ

**2.25** O Wonder! i enjoy each frolicking tiny wavelet, i am tickled by those terrible storms, i see the incessant names and forms as my own dancing shadows.

# Section 3a Answer examined for Raw

for the seeker who has just began on the path,
or
the initial state of Resourcefulness (Janaka)

Having heard appreciatively
    the joyful and
    exuberant and
    steady words
of Resourcefulness,

Wisdom (Ashtavakra) now queries with a smile:

**3.1** O Resourcefulness! Thee have strongly experienced yourself as one with this universe, and have seemingly detached the fear and pain. Thee have felt so tranquil and steady, thee have felt that absolute closeness to Brahman.

Would you still need something more? Anything?

ಀಀಀ

**3.2** For someone who is not yet so steadied as yourself, a bit of possessiveness may very well arise, if the senses catch a glimpse of something which is seemingly lucrative.

3.3 Why would a seeker who is on the path of "Soham - I am verily That Brahman" be bothered by notions of lack?

ʊʊʊ

3.4 Why would someone be tormented by lustful tendency for another and repent thereupon, when he has already told himself that the pristine Purity and exquisite Beauty is wholly himself.

ʊʊʊ

3.5 It is indeed a wonder that even a great man can fall prey to senses in a moment of unawareness.

**3.6** Somehow excitement and covetousness can arise when one thinks "one has to take care of somebody". Don't you know that no soul can be fulfilled by corrupt means?

ʊʊʊ

**3.7** How bizarre that rich men seek to bind their family to ill-gotten gains, even when they have a slight inkling that they shall forever make them slaves, that slavery shall be such soul's rebirth.

ʊʊʊ

**3.8** How uncanny that when a man has achieved greatness and control over a large empire, he tries to make his sons beggars by preventing them to earn for themselves or thinking that they cannot earn their own comforts or trying to give them more than their merit?

# Section 3b Answer pondered for a Yogi

Wisdom has closely observed the pleasant expression on the countenance of Resourcefulness and the vibrations of Janaka's mind;
and
become satisfied that all is in order,
the disciple is hugging the track.

Resourcefulness has been hearing patiently the plight of the Celebrities and the Wealthy,
whom all think to be Superior.

Wisdom senses that Resourcefulness now wishes to hear about the True Great, those who do not lose awareness even by mistake or coincidence.
Those whose sincerity is legendary, they who are the True Beloved of the Lord,
those whom the Lord Loves,

(rather than mortals puffed up by outer superiority).

Wisdom continues:

3.9 Hear about the genuine seekers on the path, who maintain humility and simplicity and spontaneity, irrespective of events and occasions.

ꕥꕥꕥ

3.10 Authenticity reflects in he who is guileless. One feels unharmed in his presence.

**3.11** His aura doesn't depress you; his presence doesn't make you feel inferior. His company banishes the fear of shame.

ඉඉඉ

**3.12** Analogy of such a seeker is rare in men; his level of contentedness is not the product of any lack, nay it is the degree of attainment of the Self.

**3.13** Such seekers are different in the sense their aura doesn't smack of need, whatever we do for them is for our own benefit.

ᗕᗕᗕ

**3.14** Know that the real man is he who doesn't get flustered from within, who doesn't seek another's wealth nor downfall; nor harp on helping someone.

Section 4 The Answer Praised

# I AM PURE. I AM WHOLE.
## Can Anyone Else Be Less Fortunate?

---

Ashtavakra expounds further:

**4.1** Truly the man of good sense lives life as a game. His thoughts and actions are too far removed from the common denizens of the world.

ϕϕϕ

**4.2** Truly the real saint doesn't feel suffocated by wealthy men around him, nor subjugated by powerful men in his vicinity.

**4.3** Truly the man of dispassion sees politics and power as cumulonimbus and cumulus clouds, that dissipate quickly, so never indulges in such talk.

ɸɸɸ

**4.4** Know that nature provides for him, nature ensures his well-being, and nature lends him a ready hand.

**4.5** He towers above the various type of men and beasts; he is unstained by avarice and untouched by phenomena.

ɸɸɸ

**4.6** Rare is he who moves without ill-will, without intent to harm the big and powerful, without notion to enslave or unite the weak.

# Section 5 The Answer Simplified

Ashtavakra states that knowledge gets grounded by shunning bad company,

whether in the family
or
without:

**5.1** How? How can you ever think of connecting with the gross? Can Gold be mixed with dirt? What superficial blemish can Gold have that needs to be removed?

Stay clear of those who give you a headache. Know they are not to be handled by you. Only then shall you feel ready for the Impossible.

000

**5.2** These people get nourished by you. They feed your brain and alter your digestion. They bubble up in your thoughts at the wrong hour. Stay clear of them and you shall be ready for Infinity.

5.3 Your senses get corroded by their company, your intellect gets clouded by their prattle, they are the dangerous snakes, lifeless when left alone. Shove them aside forthwith and feel the Grace.

ಠಠಠ

5.4 Not by their association, but by their dissociation alone shall you experience the Truth. They do not deserve your company, nor wealth, nor favor, they came close only to teach you dispassion. Be free of them and attain Brahman.

Wisdom now elucidates upon good company:

Section 6 Quest for the Genuine

MY THOUGHT CAN HEAL.
MY WORDS CAN HEAL.
MY GLANCE SURELY DOES.

**6.1** The open skies am I, with freedom to associate with the just. Noblemen can give me integrity; they can point the way to wisdom. There is no physical give and take wrt the wise, their company doesn't cause any strain. Their thoughts do my job without fuss, their presence doesn't intrude, they give no task that is a burden.

☷

**6.2** The boundless ocean I am, happy people are the sparkling waves. Their happiness shows me the way. In happiness i feel alive without strain, no needs no bonds no running away.

**6.3** The pure pearl am i, around me reflect the magnanimous. The benevolent shower blessings of peace. In peace i thrive abundantly, no fuss no crave no thorn.

ᗑᗑᗑ

**6.4** O Grace! My intellect encompasses and accepts all men and machines and ideas, plants and trees and beasts around me, and also those far away or in the news and stories. The Lord showers me with abundant love. This pristine knowledge is firmly established in my brain and heart. I feel inspired, i feel encouraged, my courage knows no bounds since my faith is deep.

Resourcefulness has been absorbing the words of
Wisdom with rapt attention
and
there has been a fountain sprouting within his heart.

Janaka exults:

# Section 7 The Genuine is near at hand

**7.1** Storms and Volcanoes erupt inside me, swirling emotions tangled with thought waves. I notice the whirlpools, i get swayed some, sometimes i begin to drown, but soon i am up and about, shouldering my responsibility with elan and charm.

ooo

**7.2** Deep in my heart, my memories sometimes stir, some people prick like thorns, some events cause upheaval, but soon they all subside.

**7.3** Hidden in the experiences of life, are situations that cause gloom and haze, and some that make me smile and sparkle, now i welcome most with patience and wonder.

ooo

**7.4** I have realized that God is not limited by my notions, nor do all my wishes qualify for Lord's blessing. With discrimination Vairagya, i have learnt to filter my demands and pacify myself, in that is my salvation.

**7.5** I see myself as Integrated and One. I sense the Presence. I feel the closeness of the Divine. Soon the curtains come down, soon the movie of ups and downs goes into the background, soon i steady myself and find life is all bliss.

ooo

Section 8  What to Avoid

# I LET GO of NOTIONS.
# I DILUTE BIAS, POLARITY.
# I ERASE MEMORY REGULARLY.

Wisdom is elated with his disciple's enlightenment, and summarizes.

Ashtavakra gives the gist:

**8.1** Bondage, imprisonment, dissatisfaction, or lack are all momentary. These are caused when one gets stuck to some "great" notion which is "irrelevant" for the occasion.

!!!

**8.2** Salvation is merging into the moment. Nirvana is "not taking adversity to heart" after its passing.

8.3 Over-indulgence in sense organ (whether going after beauty, wealth, music and discourse, prattle and passing comments, taste, smell, body contact) makes one weak. Weakness gives rise to anger, despair and ultimate self-destruction. In youth itself make a U-turn to relax the extravagance, if any, if you desire freedom later on.

!!!

8.4 It is better to leave the room where you do not belong, it is better to avoid arguments midway that turn bitter. Make the determination to not enforce your point or engage much in wrong company, even for work or business, that makes life charming.

Ashtavakra has made his point regarding what to avoid.

He continues to establish
- the Practical and
- the Subtle

points.

Section 9 Let go well in Time

**MY TRUTH IS OPEN ENDED.
MY VISION IS FAR EXTENDED.
I AM COMFORTABLE ANYWHERE.**

**9.1** Duties and Responsibilities have a scope till retirement. Retire when the body is fit, and make your mental load light, then you shall automatically sense the Presence.

~~~

**9.2** Rare is the Man who well in time relaxes his ego and hold over possessions. Do's and Don'ts should drop from your shoulders wrt others.

~~~

**9.3** Rare is the Man who attains the threefold peace - peace of his bodyMind condition, peace of environmentFamily entanglements, peace wrt workFinances.

**9.4** There is a very subtle point - hear that with earnestness. Is anyone in better condition that you? Breathe deeply - Ponder silently - and then the answer comes, "No, not really". Be grateful that you have realized this.

∼∼∼

**9.5** There is an even subtler point. All spiritual texts, all cultures, all saints wish mankind to be free, yet talk to a specific audience in a specific time-period. Best to learn from a living saint or a live satsang where you feel light-hearted and accepted.

∼∼∼

**9.6** There is now a transcendental point. Truth is multidimensional. Truth is not bound by general statements. Truth is not an object of reasoning and logic. Find the Guru who uncovers your fears so you can face them calmly, lessens your pain, dilutes your guilt or bitterness.

**9.7** Learn to look at the atoms that make up gold and clay, a beloved or the bitter fiend; gold shines forth, repulsion fades away, faith gets established.

~~~

**9.8** When your body forgets to become ill, when your mind dismisses the bothersome, know that you can go Anywhere, know that you can do Anything.

### Section 10 Moha Infatuation Lust

## MOHA is external.
## In Silence do I SEPARATE it.

The Unknown can be touched in Silence = the moments when thoughts subside, when feeling or emotions go into the background

---

Ashtavakra now hammers the energy tattva representing likes and dislikes, known as infatuation, also lust.

**10.1** Observe what you are attracted to. Observe what you are not attracted to. Observe what you are repulsed with. Also observe what you are not repulsed with.

Clearly state your likes, dislikes and neutrality. Write them down in three baskets. Over a period of 40 days, see if anything has flipped to another basket. Over 400 days, if you are truthful, surely a flip-flop that amazes you shall happen.

卐卐卐

**10.2** Most infatuations (love and hate) can be classified as:
- family members and friends
- properties of mixed ownership, assets, mementoes, gifts
- liquid cash, bank balance, gold
- notions of right and wrong, especially related to laws, government, and society
- the wife and other girls one finds agreeable

卐卐卐

**10.3** Know that strong pulls of family members are most destructive in the long run. A family was given simply as a carton or cover for protection in early days.

Do not try to stretch the family ties. Similarly, do not try to over protect your bank balance and assets and fame, as that becomes an incurable fatal illness.

Also, do not keep harping on your hatred for government or anyone, as that makes you weak and feeble.

**10.4** There is a prison made by one's likes and dislikes.

This prison is very hard to escape from.
This prison does more damage to one's soul than a jail.

卐卐卐

**10.5** The liking for a girl is natural, similarly is hatred for a jilted flame. With time it can flip-flop, so nourish your love and surrender your hate.

卐卐卐

**10.6** A Girl can be very likeable and have a strong pull, only reciprocate if you can maintain for a long time, depending upon expense and earning, else cool down and simply maintain a distant cordiality.

**10.7** Strong likes and dislikes shall drain away your liquid strength like wind carries away the moisture.

Both attraction and repulsion shall drain your sap and make you weak.

卐卐卐

**10.8** Sweet words and pretty gifts are momentary, each new day you shall have to expend in fresh expenditure and airhostess-style honeyed tongue.

Section 11 Dissociation

# Dissociation leads me to the Truth. The Unknown is Inside.

Ashtavakra provides a remedy.

**11.1** The flip-flop basket experiment is a reminder that passions change. This can turn the mind inwards to find real solace.

卐卐卐

**11.2** Within there is a whole new world that does not drain nor doth injure the soul.

卐卐卐

**11.3** Observing each passion helps dilute the impact.

Going inwards does not rob you of pleasure, rather prevents the pleasure from robbing you.

**11.4** When the currents of attraction and repulsion become somewhat balanced, one cannot be destroyed by hate, nor become a victim of undue lust.

卐卐卐

**11.5** Thinking that you shall care for your children even after they are grown up, will cause you to become a barrier to their peace and happiness, and shall also cause grief to you in turn.

So turn your efforts and money away from them and do great works for humanity.

卐卐卐

**11.6** Dissociate in time from the bodies of your family members. Dissociate spending for them and thinking of them.

Expand your vision to include humanity and your creativity and efforts shall reap immense rewards devoid of the stain of infatuation.

**11.7** In doing for family it is always insufficient, in helping humanity there is always divine blessing.

Even a bit for humanity gets counted, even infinity for infatuation is discounted.

卐卐卐

**11.8** In due course of time, know that you have done enough for family, and rest in peace wrt to them.

In due course of time turn your attention to the cosmos, and you shall attain all that you seek.

Section 12 Son to Sun

# MY First Contact with UNKNOWN.

---

Janaka has assimilated this tangential wisdom. Having mulled over it, and internalizing it, he comes to a conclusion.

**12.1** I realize that it is not needed to spend extra efforts, honeyed thoughts, or sweet words for family, beyond what i do for society.

My family is not above humanity, my family is not dearer than my country. My soul needs oneness with the world, rather than be hijacked by a small group and spend my entire life in a shell.

At the same time my faith has deepened that each contribution i make for society goes to the subtle bank balance of my family. Their souls shall also be emancipated if they honestly strive independent of my help.

ஃஃஃ

**12.2** The emotions of family no longer distract and cloud my intellect.

I had considered a tiny part of creation as mine, now my consciousness expands to the far corners of the globe.

**12.3** When i was infatuated by my family, i spent my entire day under their thumb. I was Running here and there to fend for them, to feed them, to defend even their wrong actions and habits, and became unknowingly imprisoned in their desires and expectations.

Now i am freed of such small identity, and my thoughts welcome the infinite. Now i soar in heavenly realms, now i touch the depths of samadhi.

Now i feel thoroughly relaxed, now my heart is clear of blame and guilt. Now my fitness is on track, now my vision is purified.

Now my efforts pay rich dividends. O how caring nature has become.

ঠঠঠ

**12.4** O what great exploits my actions spring, what noble deeds now erupt from my bosom.

Devoid of the limiting impulses of my limited family, the world now spurs me ever onward, humanity benefits as a whole.

**12.5** Meditation energizes my entire being, Relaxation expels all illness.

My heart now beats for the divine, my hands now extend his hands.

My yearnings heal time and space, the entire creation unites with me, my soul is forever free.

༄༄༄

**12.6** i no longer act to help my son, my actions are now applauded by the sun.

The Sun is the one who rears and cares for all sons, the Sun now protects my son, the Sun now protects my world.

**12.7** my thought is no longer blocked; my mind is free to think. I can now process multiple thoughts, i can now arrive at broad solutions.

**My thought can heal, my words can heal, my glance surely heals.**

༄༄༄

**12.8** Blessed is he who is such a one, my grateful prayerful showers for such a soul.

Blessed is me to have such company.
Blessed is i to have been born.

# Section 13 Satiated Girlfriend

# MY Joy Overflows.

---

Janaka continues to describe his exalted state of mind:

**13.1** Trust and Peace thrive in big ventures, trust and peace diminish in petty profits.

The subtle dimensions of trust and peace reveal their nature to me. The piece of land i was going to give to my niece, i ended up giving to some bright boys from college who had a bigger idea.

Tranquility dawned in me, their land and their invention cleared the debts of my city-state in no time and made the entire populace wealthy.

ʊʊʊ

**13.2** When it was needed to scold my niece or my brother it was very difficult, as their ego was painful to bear.

Now i visit the boys once in a while and we pat each other, happily enjoying the fruits that accrue to all from a small piece of land.

**13.3** I now know that God lends a hand when i shatter my shell, all great works are by his direct involvement, and all timid projects are by his indifference to jell with my smallness.

ଏଏଏଏ

**13.4** Some noble men now call upon me to discuss big tasks, even heads of state wish for my counsel.

I tread these tracks carefully, avoiding undue wealth proposals.

I focus more on clean energy and ecofriendly projects, i know my vision shall find nature's support and be carried forth long after i bid adieu to the planet.

**13.5** Guilt and fear and illness no longer target me, they give me a wide berth, they are now wary of me, they move aside to let me pass, their absence is starkly evident.

ಉಉಉ

**13.6** Even my family and friends have now turned in my support, i sense the veil has lifted from their souls, i feel blessed the divine has not forsaken them.

ಉಉಉ

**13.7** Even my wife and my girlfriends and the women i liked, all seem to have been granted peace and prosperity, all are now at ease, all are well settled in good society.

Their talents have blossomed, their soul finds solace.

Section 14 Peace Solidifies

# MY Wishes are GRANTED.

Janaka continues in a state of deep peace, his heart molten love:

**14.1** Since the ties of craving for bodies, whether near ones or physical objects, has diminished, my mind has become free to download subtle secrets.

༄༄༄

**14.2** My mind is now free to think beyond the mundane, and it can see the possibilities in nature that extend the planes of knowledge. That can help build inventions of immense utility.

༄༄༄

**14.3** I can witness the infinite and its ways, i can realize my potential to function beyond laws and create beyond temporal boundaries.

**14.4** O i wish communion with the enlightened, i wish the company of the wise, i wish to be amongst those who are unaffected by government and society.

I seek them who work without getting deluded by emotions around them.

I know i shall have my wish granted, i know i shall do works that shall stand the test of time. I know my inventions shall set the trend for mankind, i know my ideas shall break the shackles of moha for the brave and the brilliant.

I wish to be remembered as the gallant who served society, not as the one who got consumed by filial desire.

Section 15 Be Bold yet Natural

# Divine becomes MY Friend.

Wisdom responds to his disciple with a gaze that showers grace, a glance that reconfigures the physical laws to accommodate a man of unparalleled humanness.

**15.1** I see that you have listened with attention, and expressed with devotion. These are rare. These are rare.

Attentiveness is rare because men are already full to the brim with information, concepts and bias.

Devotion is lacking because each man claims he already has a past master, he is already praying to an invisible God. What need for living human saints they ask?

**15.2** Direct your senses to become aware of the physical laws and the possibilities of tuning them for benevolence.

Again and again acknowledge the presence of the Lord who has made you unique and talented to do great inventions.

Rise above weakness and profanity, nourish the strong and lend a helping hand to the brave.

**15.3** Vivacity and sociability have their place in the world, but only in childhood and youth.

As you grow in strength and wisdom, seek out silence and meditation, for this knowledge is an inner wealth, and cannot be transmitted via public broadcast.

Again and again go solitary, again and again dissolve in nature. Let the purity and tranquility rub off on you, let the air and space speak to you.

**15.4** You are bigger than your body, your might far exceeds this timid frame. You can create galaxies; you can power cities by thought alone.

You are free to achieve what you will. What shall you WILL knowing this?

Will the highest, live the fullest, tower above the man machine.

**15.5** Your family will come, the neighbor will come, the government shall come to beg of you. Big men shall come, bigger ideas they shall try to sell to you.

Treat it as business divine, help those who stick to Truth, Hard Work and Honesty.

༄༅༅

**15.6** See their ignorance and steer clear of them, not by their glib association can you function.

The Lord resides in one and all, but you cannot reach out to those whose lord is fast asleep.

Let nature first awaken those men who qualify for wisdom. Do your part then.

༄༅༅

**15.7** At the same time know that each seed blossoms in a particular space at a particular time.

Let not your munificence leak out to those yet unworthy, their time shall come in due course, patience is a golden rule.

**15.8** Trust yourself, have faith in the divine presence, know success kisses your feet anon.

Nature is there to side with you, the physical forces are willing to befriend you, time is ready to reveal its secrets, the Lord wishes you wealth and wisdom.

**15.9** Your parents have departed, your children shall also go, they filled you with emotion, be ever grateful.

**15.10** Your body is precious, an irreplaceable gift. Treat it with understanding, do your part to keep it fit.

A cheerful mind is made divine by a fit Body. A creative mind is showered with grace when it listens to the body. You can do wonders when both mind and body are soaked in the divine.

༄༅༄

**15.11** Plan your routine to accommodate your body's needs of exercise, food and sleep.

The biorhythm of each body is different, do not enforce static laws of discipline.

Move with the times, mix with the cultures, allow nature to be natural.

**15.12** The seasons have a message, each sunset, moonrise, and high tide has a rhythm. Be separate, yet inseparable.

---

**15.13** Your birth is no ordinary event.

Your birth has sent waves of joy pulsating through the galaxies, you have made the stars dance and your coming has made time proud.

---

**15.14** Your brilliance marks the silver lining of the clouds, nay, your sparks are the veritable dance of lightning.

You are the sun that turns snow clad mountain peaks to gold. That spectacle can heal tourists who glance at them.

**15.15** Feel the nature deep inside, feel the oneness with the mountains and roads, with the rivers and electric poles.

You are much more than your frame, your consciousness is what powers the sun and makes life and relationships possible.

॰॰॰

**15.16** You enjoy the sattva that causes liberation, you are not averse to the tamas that causes bondage.

The play and interplay of both is called life and death, both are inevitable, neither is expendable.

**15.17** Remember each notion is temporary, each concept and theory applies to an infinitesimal part of time and space.

That is why the language of saints' changes with culture, era, and geography.

That is why a living master delivers what no past master can, nay each master is successively reborn to address a tiny populace, and of that slice if one or two attain divine union, the reverberations echo across the galaxies, all get a drop of nectar, the play continues.

༺༻

**15.18** In this world if you can touch one life, know you are very fortunate.

If one more can find the realization through you, know that you are most fortunate.

Know that you made the Lord happy. Know that his happiness causes bliss for all, know that he who pleases the lord becomes immortal.

**15.19** You and the Lord are not separate, but as if separate.

For play the Lord made you, sometimes he wins, at other times he ensures your victory.

But when you merge in him when still alive, then you enjoy the spectacle from his eyes.

☙❧

**15.20** Overthink NOT, Relax OFTEN.

# Latin Transliteration Chart

International Alphabet of Sanskrit Transliteration (I.A.S.T.)

| a | ā | i | ī | u | ū | ṛ | ṝ | ḷ | |
|---|---|---|---|---|---|---|---|---|---|
| अ | आ | इ | ई | उ | ऊ | ऋ | ॠ | ऌ | |
| | | | | | | | | | |
| e | ai | o | au | ṃ | m̐ | ḥ | Ardha Visarga | oṃ | |
| ए | ऐ | ओ | औ | ं | ँ | ः | ▢ | ॐ | |
| Consonants are shown with vowel 'a= अ' for uttering | | | | | | | | | |
| ka | क | ca | च | ṭa | ट | ta | त | pa | प |
| kha | ख | cha | छ | ṭha | ठ | tha | थ | pha | फ |
| ga | ग | ja | ज | ḍa | ड | da | द | ba | ब |
| gha | घ | jha | झ | ḍha | ढ | dha | ध | bha | भ |
| ṅa | ङ | ña | ञ | ṇa | ण | na | न | ma | म |
| ya | ra | la | va | ḻa | ' | | | | |
| य | र | ल | व | ळ | S | | | | |
| | | | | **Consonant only** | | | | | |
| śa | ṣa | sa | ha | ka | क्अ = क | | | | |
| श | ष | स | ह | k | क् | | | | |

The symbol ⁎ is pronounced as गुं guṃ. It is an ayogavaha अयोगवाह sound seen in Vedic literature due to Sandhi.

# Sanskrit Verses for Chanting

Ashtavakara Gita is written in Anushtup Chanda. Each verse consists of 32 syllables, each statement (half verse) consists of 16 syllables. While chanting, we pause at a quarter verse, i.e. at 8 syllables.

॥ अथ अष्टावक्र गीता ॥

1 प्रथमं प्रकरणम् । जनक उवाच ।
कथं ज्ञानम् अवाप्नोति कथं मुक्तिर्भविष्यति ।
वैराग्यं च कथं प्राप्तं एतद् ब्रूहि मम प्रभो ॥ 1.1 ॥ 1

अष्टावक्र उवाच ।
मुक्तिम् इच्छसि चेत् तात विषयान् विषवत् त्यज ।
क्षमार्जवदयातोषसत्यं पीयूषवद् भज ॥ 1.2 ॥ 2

न पृथ्वी न जलं नाग्निर् न वायुर् द्यौर् न वा भवान् ।
एषां साक्षिणमात्मानं चिद् रूपं विद्धि मुक्तये ॥ 1.3 ॥ 3

यदि देहं पृथक् कृत्य चिति विश्राम्य तिष्ठसि ।
अधुनैव सुखी शान्तो बन्धमुक्तो भविष्यसि ॥ 1.4 ॥ 4

न त्वं विप्रादिको वर्णो नाश्रमी नाक्षगोचरः ।
असङ्गोऽसि निराकारो विश्वसाक्षी सुखी भव ॥ 1.5 ॥ 5

धर्माधर्मौ सुखं दुःखं मानसानि न ते विभो ।
न कर्तासि न भोक्तासि मुक्त एवासि सर्वदा ॥ 1.6 ॥ 6

एको द्रष्टासि सर्वस्य मुक्तप्रायोऽसि सर्वदा ।
अयमेव हि ते बन्धो द्रष्टारं पश्यसीतरम् ॥ 1.7 ॥ 7

अहं कर्तेत्यहंमानमहाकृष्णाहिदंशितः ।
नाहं कर्तेति विश्वासामृतं पीत्वा सुखी भव ॥ 1.8 ॥ 8

एको विशुद्धबोधोऽहम् इति निश्चयवह्निना ।
प्रज्वाल्याज्ञानगहनं वीतशोकः सुखी भव ॥ 1.9 ॥ 9

यत्र विश्वमिदं भाति कल्पितं रज्जुसर्पवत् ।
आनन्दपरमानन्दः स बोधस्त्वं सुखं चर ॥ 1.10 ॥ 10

मुक्ताभिमानी मुक्तो हि बद्धो बद्धाभिमान्यपि ।
किंवदन्तीह सत्येयं या मतिः सा गतिर् भवेत् ॥ 1.11 ॥ 11

आत्मा साक्षी विभुः पूर्ण एको मुक्तश्चिदक्रियः ।
असङ्गो निःस्पृहः शान्तो भ्रमात् संसारवानिव ॥ 1.12 ॥ 12

कूटस्थं बोधमद्वैतमात्मानं परिभावय ।
आभासोऽहं भ्रमं मुक्त्वा भावं बाह्यमथान्तरम् ॥ 1.13 ॥ 13

देहाभिमानपाशेन चिरं बद्धोऽसि पुत्रक ।
बोधोऽहं ज्ञानखङ्गेन तन्निष्कृत्य सुखी भव ॥ 1.14 ॥ 14

निःसङ्गो निष्क्रियोऽसि त्वं स्वप्रकाशो निरञ्जनः ।
अयमेव हि ते बन्धः समाधिमनुतिष्ठसि ॥ 1.15 ॥ 15

त्वया व्याप्तमिदं विश्वं त्वयि प्रोतं यथार्थतः ।
शुद्धबुद्धस्वरूपस्त्वं मा गमः क्षुद्रचित्तताम् ॥ 1.16 ॥ 16

निरपेक्षो निर्विकारो निर्भरः शीतलाशयः ।
अगाधबुद्धिरक्षुब्धो भव चिन्मात्रवासनः ॥ 1.17 ॥ 17

साकारमनृतं विद्धि निराकारं तु निश्चलम् ।
एतत् तत्त्वोपदेशेन न पुनर्भवसम्भवः ॥ 1.18 ॥ 18

यथैवादर्शमध्यस्थे रूपेऽन्तः परितस्तु सः ।
तथैवाऽस्मिन् शरीरेऽन्तः परितः परमेश्वरः ॥ 1.19 ॥ 19

एकं सर्वगतं व्योम बहिरन्तर्यथा घटे ।
नित्यं निरन्तरं ब्रह्म सर्वभूतगणे तथा ॥ 1.20 ॥ 20


2 द्वितीयं प्रकरणम् । जनक उवाच ।
अहो निरञ्जनः शान्तो बोधोऽहं प्रकृतेः परः ।
एतावन्तमहं कालं मोहेनैव विडम्बितः ॥ 2.1 ॥ 21

यथा प्रकाशयाम्येको देहमेनं तथा जगत् ।
अतो मम जगत् सर्वमथवा न च किञ्चन ॥ 2.2 ॥ 22

सशरीरमहो विश्वं परित्यज्य मयाऽधुना ।
कुतश्चित् कौशलादेव परमात्मा विलोक्यते ॥ 2.3 ॥ 23

यथा न तोयतो भिन्नास्तरङ्गाः फेनबुद्बुदाः ।
आत्मनो न तथा भिन्नं विश्वमात्मविनिर्गतम् ॥ 2.4 ॥ 24

तन्तुमात्रो भवेदेव पटो यद्वद्विचारितः ।
आत्मतन्मात्रमेवेदं तद्वद्विश्वं विचारितम् ॥ 2.5 ॥ 25

यथैवेक्षुरसे क्लृप्ता तेन व्याप्तैव शर्करा ।
तथा विश्वं मयि क्लृप्तं मया व्याप्तं निरन्तरम् ॥ 2.6 ॥ 26

आत्मज्ञानाज्जगद् भाति आत्मज्ञानान्न भासते ।
रज्जुज्ञानादहिर्भाति तज्ज्ञानाद् भासते न हि ॥ 2.7 ॥ 27

प्रकाशो मे निजं रूपं नातिरिक्तोऽस्म्यहं ततः ।
यदा प्रकाशते विश्वं तदाऽहं भास एव हि ॥ 2.8 ॥ 28

अहो विकल्पितं विश्वमज्ञानान्मयि भासते ।
रूप्यं शुक्तौ फणी रज्जौ वारि सूर्यकरे यथा ॥ 2.9 ॥ 29

मत्तो विनिर्गतं विश्वं मय्येव लयमेष्यति ।
मृदि कुम्भो जले वीचिः कनके कटकं यथा ॥ 2.10 ॥ 30

अहो अहं नमो मह्यं विनाशो यस्य नास्ति मे ।
ब्रह्मादिस्तम्बपर्यन्तं जगन्नाशोऽपि तिष्ठतः ॥ 2.11 ॥ 31

अहो अहं नमो मह्यं एकोऽहं देहवानपि ।
क्वचिन्न गन्ता नागन्ता व्याप्य विश्वमवस्थितः ॥ 2.12 ॥ 32

अहो अहं नमो मह्यं दक्षो नास्तीह मत्समः ।
असंस्पृश्य शरीरेण येन विश्वं चिरं धृतम् ॥ 2.13 ॥ 33

अहो अहं नमो मह्यं यस्य मे नास्ति किञ्चन ।
अथवा यस्य मे सर्वं यद् वाङ्मनसगोचरम् ॥ 2.14 ॥ 34

ज्ञानं ज्ञेयं तथा ज्ञाता त्रितयं नास्ति वास्तवम् ।
अज्ञानाद् भाति यत्रेदं सोऽहमस्मि निरञ्जनः ॥ 2.15 ॥ 35

द्वैतमूलमहो दुःखं नान्यत्तस्यास्ति भेषजम् ।
दृश्यमेतन्मृषा सर्वमेकोऽहं चिद्रसोऽमलः ॥ 2.16 ॥ 36

बोधमात्रोऽहमज्ञानाद् उपाधिः कल्पितो मया ।
एवं विमृशतो नित्यं निर्विकल्पे स्थितिर्मम ॥ 2.17 ॥ 37

न मे बन्धोऽस्ति मोक्षो वा भ्रान्तिः शान्ता निराश्रया ।
अहो मयि स्थितं विश्वं वस्तुतो न मयि स्थितम् ॥ 2.18 ॥ 38

सशरीरमिदं विश्वं न किञ्चिदिति निश्चितम् ।
शुद्धचिन्मात्र आत्मा च तत्कस्मिन् कल्पनाधुना ॥ 2.19 ॥ 39

शरीरं स्वर्गनरकौ बन्धमोक्षौ भयं तथा ।
कल्पनामात्रमेवैतत् किं मे कार्यं चिदात्मनः ॥ 2.20 ॥ 40

अहो जनसमूहेऽपि न द्वैतं पश्यतो मम ।
अरण्यमिव संवृत्तं क्व रतिं करवाण्यहम् ॥ 2.21 ॥ 41

नाहं देहो न मे देहो जीवो नाहमहं हि चित् ।
अयमेव हि मे बन्ध आसीद्या जीविते स्पृहा ॥ 2.22 ॥ 42

अहो भुवनकल्लोलैर्विचित्रैर्द्राक् समुत्थितम् ।
मय्यनन्तमहाम्भोधौ चित्तवाते समुद्यते ॥ 2.23 ॥ 43

मय्यनन्तमहाम्भोधौ चित्तवाते प्रशाम्यति ।
अभाग्याज्जीववणिजो जगत्पोतो विनश्वरः ॥ 2.24 ॥ 44

मय्यनन्तमहाम्भोधावाश्चर्यं जीववीचयः ।
उद्यन्ति घ्नन्ति खेलन्ति प्रविशन्ति स्वभावतः ॥ 2.25 ॥ 45

3 तृतीयं प्रकरणम् । अष्टावक्र उवाच ।
अविनाशिनमात्मानमेकं विज्ञाय तत्त्वतः ।
तवात्मज्ञस्य धीरस्य कथमर्थार्जने रतिः ॥ 3.1 ॥ 46

आत्माज्ञानादहो प्रीतिर्विषयभ्रमगोचरे ।
शुक्तेरज्ञानतो लोभो यथा रजतविभ्रमे ॥ 3.2 ॥ 47

विश्वं स्फुरति यत्रेदं तरङ्गा इव सागरे ।
सोऽहमस्मीति विज्ञाय किं दीन इव धावसि ॥ 3.3 ॥ 48

श्रुत्वाऽपि शुद्धचैतन्यम् आत्मानमतिसुन्दरम् ।
उपस्थेऽत्यन्तसंसक्तो मालिन्यमधिगच्छति ॥ 3.4 ॥ 49

सर्वभूतेषु चात्मानं सर्वभूतानि चात्मनि ।
मुनेर्जानत आश्चर्यं ममत्वमनुवर्तते ॥ 3.5 ॥ 50

आस्थितः परमाद्वैतं मोक्षार्थेऽपि व्यवस्थितः ।
आश्चर्यं कामवशगो विकलः केलिशिक्षया ॥ 3.6 ॥ 51

उद्भूतं ज्ञानदुर्मित्रमवधार्यातिदुर्बलः ।
आश्चर्यं काममाकाङ्क्षेत् कालमन्तमनुश्रितः ॥ 3.7 ॥ 52

इहामुत्र विरक्तस्य नित्यानित्यविवेकिनः ।
आश्चर्यं मोक्षकामस्य मोक्षादेव विभीषिका ॥ 3.8 ॥ 53

धीरस्तु भोज्यमानोऽपि पीड्यमानोऽपि सर्वदा ।
आत्मानं केवलं पश्यन् न तुष्यति न कुप्यति ॥ 3.9 ॥ 54

चेष्टमानं शरीरं स्वं पश्यत्यन्यशरीरवत् ।
संस्तवे चापि निन्दायां कथं क्षुभ्येत् महाशयः ॥ 3.10 ॥ 55

मायामात्रमिदं विश्वं पश्यन् विगतकौतुकः ।
अपि सन्निहिते मृत्यौ कथं त्रस्यति धीरधीः ॥ 3.11 ॥ 56

निःस्पृहं मानसं यस्य नैराश्येऽपि महात्मनः ।
तस्यात्मज्ञानतृप्तस्य तुलना केन जायते ॥ 3.12 ॥ 57

स्वभावादेव जानानो दृश्यमेतन्न किञ्चन ।
इदं ग्राह्यमिदं त्याज्यं स किं पश्यति धीरधीः ॥ 3.13 ॥ 58

अन्तस्त्यक्तकषायस्य निर्द्वन्द्वस्य निराशिषः ।
यदृच्छयागतो भोगो न दुःखाय न तुष्टये ॥ 3.14 ॥ 59

## 4 चतुर्थं प्रकरणम् । अष्टावक्र उवाच ।

हन्तात्मज्ञस्य धीरस्य खेलतो भोगलीलया ।
न हि संसारवाहीकैर्मूढैः सह समानता ॥ 4.1 ॥ 60

यत् पदं प्रेप्सवो दीनाः शक्राद्याः सर्वदेवताः ।
अहो तत्र स्थितो योगी न हर्षमुपगच्छति ॥ 4.2 ॥ 61

तज्ज्ञस्य पुण्यपापाभ्यां स्पर्शो ह्यन्तर्न जायते ।
न ह्याकाशस्य धूमेन दृश्यमानापि सङ्गतिः ॥ 4.3 ॥ 62

आत्मैवेदं जगत्सर्वं ज्ञातं येन महात्मना ।
यदृच्छया वर्तमानं तं निषेद्धुं क्षमेत कः ॥ 4.4 ॥ 63

आब्रह्मस्तम्बपर्यन्ते भूतग्रामे चतुर्विधे ।
विज्ञस्यैव हि सामर्थ्यमिच्छानिच्छाविवर्जने ॥ 4.5 ॥ 64

आत्मानमद्वयं कश्चिज्जानाति जगदीश्वरम् ।
यद् वेत्ति तत् स कुरुते न भयं तस्य कुत्रचित् ॥ 4.6 ॥ 65

## 5 पञ्चमं प्रकरणम् । अष्टावक्र उवाच ।

न ते सङ्गोऽस्ति केनापि किं शुद्धस्त्यक्तुमिच्छसि ।
सङ्घातविलयं कुर्वन्नेवमेव लयं व्रज ॥ 5.1 ॥ 66

उदेति भवतो विश्वं वारिधेरिव बुद्बुदः ।
इति ज्ञात्वैकमात्मानं एवमेव लयं व्रज ॥ 5.2 ॥ 67

प्रत्यक्षमप्यवस्तुत्वाद् विश्वं नास्त्यमले त्वयि ।
रज्जुसर्प इव व्यक्तं एवमेव लयं व्रज ॥ 5.3 ॥ 68

समदुःखसुखः पूर्ण आशानैराश्ययोः समः ।
समजीवितमृत्युः सन्नेवमेव लयं व्रज ॥ 5.4 ॥ 69

<u>6 षष्ठं प्रकरणम् । अष्टावक्र उवाच ।</u>
आकाशवदनन्तोऽहं घटवत् प्राकृतं जगत् ।
इति ज्ञानं तथैतस्य न त्यागो न ग्रहो लयः ॥ 6.1 ॥ 70

महोदधिरिवाऽहं स प्रपञ्चो वीचिसऽन्निभः ।
इति ज्ञानं तथैतस्य न त्यागो न ग्रहो लयः ॥ 6.2 ॥ 71

अहं स शुक्तिसङ्काशो रूप्यवद् विश्वकल्पना ।
इति ज्ञानं तथैतस्य न त्यागो न ग्रहो लयः ॥ 6.3 ॥ 72

अहं वा सर्वभूतेषु सर्वभूतान्यथो मयि ।
इति ज्ञानं तथैतस्य न त्यागो न ग्रहो लयः ॥ 6.4 ॥ 73

<u>7 सप्तमं प्रकरणम् । जनक उवाच ।</u>
मय्यनन्तमहाम्भोधौ विश्वपोत इतस्ततः ।
भ्रमति स्वान्तवातेन न ममास्त्यसहिष्णुता ॥ 7.1 ॥ 74

मय्यनन्तमहाम्भोधौ जगद्वीचिः स्वभावतः ।
उदेतु वास्तमायातु न मे वृद्धिर्न च क्षतिः ॥ 7.2 ॥ 75

मय्यनन्तमहाम्भोधौ विश्वं नाम विकल्पना ।
अतिशान्तो निराकार एतदेवाहमास्थितः ॥ 7.3 ॥ 76

नात्मा भावेषु नो भावस्तत्रानन्ते निरञ्जने ।
इत्यसक्तोऽस्पृहः शान्त एतदेवाहमास्थितः ॥ 7.4 ॥ 77

अहो चिन्मात्रमेवाहं इन्द्रजालोपमं जगत् ।
अतो मम कथं कुत्र हेयोपादेयकल्पना ॥ 7.5 ॥ 78

## 8 अष्टमं प्रकरणम् । अष्टावक्र उवाच ।

तदा बन्धो यदा चित्तं किञ्चिद् वाञ्छति शोचति ।
किञ्चिन् मुञ्चति गृह्णाति किञ्चिद् हृष्यति कुप्यति ॥ 8.1 ॥ 79

तदा मुक्तिर्यदा चित्तं न वाञ्छति न शोचति ।
न मुञ्चति न गृह्णाति न हृष्यति न कुप्यति ॥ 8.2 ॥ 80

तदा बन्धो यदा चित्तं सक्तं कास्वपि दृष्टिषु ।
तदा मोक्षो यदा चित्तमसक्तं सर्वदृष्टिषु ॥ 8.3 ॥ 81

यदा नाहं तदा मोक्षो यदाहं बन्धनं तदा ।
मत्वेति हेलया किञ्चित् मा गृहाण विमुञ्च मा ॥ 8.4 ॥ 82

## 9 नवमं प्रकरण । अष्टावक्र उवाच ।

कृताकृते च द्वन्द्वानि कदा शान्तानि कस्य वा ।
एवं ज्ञा त्वेह निर्वेदाद् भव त्यागपरोऽव्रती ॥ 9.1 ॥ 83

कस्यापि तात धन्यस्य लोकचेष्टावलोकनात् ।
जीवितेच्छा बुभुक्षा च बुभुत्सोपशमं गता ॥ 9.2 ॥ 84

अनित्यं सर्वमेवेदं तापत्रयदूषितम् ।
असारं निन्दितं हेयमिति निश्चित्य शाम्यति ॥ 9.3 ॥ 85

कोऽसौ कालो वयः किं वा यत्र द्वन्द्वानि नो नृणाम् ।
तान्युपेक्ष्य यथाप्राप्तवर्ती सिद्धिमवाप्नुयात् ॥ 9.4 ॥ 86

नाना मतं महर्षीणां साधूनां योगिनां तथा ।
दृष्ट्वा निर्वेदमापन्नः को न शाम्यति मानवः ॥ 9.5 ॥ 87

कृत्वा मूर्तिपरिज्ञानं चैतन्यस्य न किं गुरुः ।
निर्वेदसमतायुक्त्या यस्तारयति संसृतेः ॥ 9.6 ॥ 88

पश्य भूतविकारांस्त्वं भूतमात्रान् यथार्थतः ।
तत्क्षणाद् बन्धनिर्मुक्तः स्वरूपस्थो भविष्यसि ॥ 9.7 ॥ 89

वासना एव संसार इति सर्वा विमुञ्च ताः ।
तत्त्यागो वासनात्यागात् स्थितिरद्य यथा तथा ॥ 9.8 ॥ 90

<u>10 दशमं प्रकरणम् । अष्टावक्र उवाच ।</u>
विहाय वैरिणं काममर्थं चानर्थसङ्कुलम् ।
धर्ममप्येतयोर्हेतुं सर्वत्रानादरं कुरु ॥ 10.1 ॥ 91

स्वप्नेन्द्रजालवत् पश्य दिनानि त्रीणि पञ्च वा ।
मित्रक्षेत्रधनागारदारदायादिसम्पदः ॥ 10.2 ॥ 92

यत्र यत्र भवेत्तृष्णा संसारं विद्धि तत्र वै ।
प्रौढवैराग्यमाश्रित्य वीततृष्णः सुखी भव ॥ 10.3 ॥ 93

तृष्णामात्रात्मको बन्धस्तन्नाशो मोक्ष उच्यते ।
भवासंसक्तिमात्रेण प्राप्तितुष्टिर्मुहुर्मुहुः ॥ 10.4 ॥ 94

त्वमेकश्चेतनः शुद्धो जडं विश्वमसत्तथा ।
अविद्यापि न किञ्चित्सा का बुभुत्सा तथापि ते ॥ 10.5 ॥ 95

राज्यं सुताः कलत्राणि शरीराणि सुखानि च ।
संसक्तस्यापि नष्टानि तव जन्मनि जन्मनि ॥ 10.6 ॥ 96

अलमर्थेन कामेन सुकृतेनापि कर्मणा ।
एभ्यः संसारकान्तारे न विश्रान्तमभून् मनः ॥ 10.7 ॥ 97

कृतं न कति जन्मानि कायेन मनसा गिरा ।
दुःखमायासदं कर्म तद्द्याप्युपरम्यताम् ॥ 10.8 ॥ 98

11 एकादशं प्रकरणम् । अष्टावक्र उवाच ।
भावाभावविकारश्च स्वभावादिति निश्चयी ।
निर्विकारो गतक्लेशः सुखेनैवोपशाम्यति ॥ 11.1 ॥ 99

ईश्वरः सर्वनिर्माता नेहान्य इति निश्चयी ।

अन्तर्गलितसर्वाशः शान्तः क्वापि न सज्जते ॥ 11.2 ॥ 100

आपदः सम्पदः काले दैवादेवेति निश्चयी ।
तृप्तः स्वस्थेन्द्रियो नित्यं न वाञ्छति न शोचति ॥ 11.3 ॥ 101

सुखदुःखे जन्ममृत्यू दैवादेवेति निश्चयी ।
साध्यादर्शी निरायासः कुर्वन्नपि न लिप्यते ॥ 11.4 ॥ 102

चिन्तया जायते दुःखं नान्यथेहेति निश्चयी ।
तया हीनः सुखी शान्तः सर्वत्र गलितस्पृहः ॥ 11.5 ॥ 103

नाहं देहो न मे देहो बोधोऽहमिति निश्चयी ।
कैवल्यमिव सम्प्राप्तो न स्मरत्यकृतं कृतम् ॥ 11.6 ॥ 104

आब्रह्मस्तम्बपर्यन्तं अहमेवेति निश्चयी ।
निर्विकल्पः शुचिः शान्तः प्राप्ताप्राप्तविनिर्वृतः ॥ 11.7 ॥ 105

नानाश्चर्यमिदं विश्वं न किञ्चिदिति निश्चयी ।
निर्वासनः स्फूर्तिमात्रो न किञ्चिदिव शाम्यति ॥ 11.8 ॥ 106

## 12 द्वादशोऽध्यायः जनक उवाच ॥
कायकृत्यासहः पूर्वं ततो वाग्विस्तरासहः ।
अथ चिन्तासहस्तस्माद् एवमेवाहमास्थितः ॥ 12.1 ॥ 107

प्रीत्यभावेन शब्दादेरदृश्यत्वेन चात्मनः ।
विक्षेपैकाग्रहृदय एवमेवाहमास्थितः ॥ 12.2 ॥ 108

समाध्यासादिविक्षिप्तौ व्यवहारः समाधये ।
एवं विलोक्य नियमम् एवमेवाहमास्थितः ॥ 12.3 ॥ 109

हेयोपादेयविरहादेवं हर्षविषादयोः ।
अभावादद्य हे ब्रह्मन् एवमेवाहमास्थितः ॥ 12.4 ॥ 110

आश्रमानाश्रमं ध्यानं चित्तस्वीकृतवर्जनं ।
विकल्पं मम वीक्ष्यैतैः एवमेवाहमास्थितः ॥ 12.5 ॥ 111

कर्मानुष्ठानमज्ञानाद् यथैवोपरमस्तथा ।
बुध्वा सम्यगिदं तत्त्वम् एवमेवाहमास्थितः ॥ 12.6 ॥ 112

अचिन्त्यं चिन्त्यमानोऽपि चिन्तारूपं भजत्यसौ ।
त्यक्त्वा तद्भावनं तस्माद् एवमेवाहमास्थितः ॥ 12.7 ॥ 113

एवमेव कृतं येन स कृतार्थो भवेदसौ ।
एवमेव स्वभावो यः स कृतार्थो भवेदसौ ॥ 12.8 ॥ 114

<u>13 त्रयोदशं प्रकरणम् । जनक उवाच ।</u>
अकिञ्चनभवं स्वास्थ्यं कौपीनत्वेऽपि दुर्लभम् ।
त्यागादाने विहायास्मादहमासे यथासुखम् ॥ 13.1 ॥ 115

कुत्रापि खेदः कायस्य जिह्वा कुत्रापि खिद्यते ।
मनः कुत्रापि तत्त्यक्त्वा पुरुषार्थे स्थितः सुखम् ॥ 13.2 ॥ 116

कृतं किमपि नैव स्याद् इति सञ्चिन्त्य तत्त्वतः ।
यदा यत्कर्तुमायाति तत् कृत्वासे यथासुखम् ॥ 13.3 ॥ 117

कर्मनैष्कर्म्यनिर्बन्धभावा देहस्थयोगिनः ।
संयोगायोगविरहादहमासे यथासुखम् ॥ 13.4 ॥ 118

अर्थानर्थौ न मे स्थित्या गत्या न शयनेन वा ।
तिष्ठन् गच्छन् स्वपन् तस्माद् अहमासे यथासुखम् ॥ 13.5 ॥ 119

स्वपतो नास्ति मे हानिः सिद्धिर्यत्नवतो न वा ।
नाशोल्लासौ विहायास्मद् अहमासे यथासुखम् ॥ 13.6 ॥ 120

सुखादिरूपा नियमं भावेष्वालोक्य भूरिशः ।
शुभाशुभे विहायास्माद् अहमासे यथासुखम् ॥ 13.7 ॥ 121

## 14 चतुर्दशं प्रकरणम् । जनक उवाच ।

प्रकृत्या शून्यचित्तो यः प्रमादाद् भावभावनः ।
निद्रितो बोधित इव क्षीणसंस्मरणो हि सः ॥ 14.1 ॥ 122

क्व धनानि क्व मित्राणि क्व मे विषयदस्यवः ।
क्व शास्त्रं क्व च विज्ञानं यदा मे गलिता स्पृहा ॥ 14.2 ॥ 123

विज्ञाते साक्षिपुरुषे परमात्मनि चेश्वरे ।
नैराश्ये बन्धमोक्षे च न चिन्ता मुक्तये मम ॥ 14.3 ॥ 124

अन्तर्विकल्पशून्यस्य बहिः स्वच्छन्दचारिणः ।
भ्रान्तस्येव दशास्तास्ताः तादृशा एव जानते ॥ 14.4 ॥ 125

## 15 पञ्चदशं प्रकरणम् । अष्टावक्र उवाच ।

यथातथोपदेशेन कृतार्थः सत्त्वबुद्धिमान् ।
आजीवमपि जिज्ञासुः परस्तत्र विमुह्यति ॥ 15.1 ॥ 126

मोक्षो विषयवैरस्यं बन्धो वैषयिको रसः ।
एतावदेव विज्ञानं यथेच्छसि तथा कुरु ॥ 15.2 ॥ 127

वाग्मिप्राज्ञमहोद्योगं जनं मूकजडालसम् ।
करोति तत्त्वबोधोऽयमतस्त्यक्तो बुभुक्षुभिः ॥ 15.3 ॥ 128

न त्वं देहो न ते देहो भोक्ता कर्ता न वा भवान् ।
चिद्रूपोऽसि सदा साक्षी निरपेक्षः सुखं चर ॥ 15.4 ॥ 129

रागद्वेषौ मनोधर्मौ न मनस्ते कदाचन ।
निर्विकल्पोऽसि बोधात्मा निर्विकारः सुखं चर ॥ 15.5 ॥ 130

सर्वभूतेषु चात्मानं सर्वभूतानि चात्मनि ।
विज्ञाय निरहंकारो निर्ममस्त्वं सुखी भव ॥ 15.6 ॥ 131

विश्वं स्फुरति यत्रेदं तरङ्गा इव सागरे ।
तत्त्वमेव न सन्देहश्चिन्मूर्ते विज्वरो भव ॥ 15.7 ॥ 132

श्रद्धस्व तात श्रद्धस्व नात्र मोहं कुरुष्व भोः ।
ज्ञानस्वरूपो भगवानात्मा त्वं प्रकृतेः परः ॥ 15.8 ॥ 133

गुणैः संवेष्टितो देहस्तिष्ठत्यायाति याति च ।

आत्मा न गन्ता नागन्ता किमेनमनुशोचसि ॥ 15.9 ॥ 134

देहस्तिष्ठतु कल्पान्तं गच्छत्वद्यैव वा पुनः ।
क्व वृद्धिः क्व च वा हानिस्तव चिन्मात्ररूपिणः ॥ 15.10 ॥ 135

त्वय्यनन्तमहाम्भोधौ विश्ववीचिः स्वभावतः ।
उदेतु वास्तमायातु न ते वृद्धिर्न वा क्षतिः ॥ 15.11 ॥ 136

तात चिन्मात्ररूपोऽसि न ते भिन्नमिदं जगत् ।
अतः कस्य कथं कुत्र हेयोपादेयकल्पना ॥ 15.12 ॥ 137

एकस्मिन्नव्यये शान्ते चिदाकाशेऽमले त्वयि ।
कुतो जन्म कुतो कर्म कुतोऽहंकार एव च ॥ 15.13 ॥ 138

यत्त्वं पश्यसि तत्रैकस्त्वमेव प्रतिभाससे ।
किं पृथक् भासते स्वर्णात् कटकाङ्गदनूपुरम् ॥ 15.14 ॥ 139

अयं सोऽहमयं नाहं विभागमिति सन्त्यज ।
सर्वमात्मेति निश्चित्य निःसङ्कल्पः सुखी भव ॥ 15.15 ॥ 140

तवैवाज्ञानतो विश्वं त्वमेकः परमार्थतः ।
त्वत्तोऽन्यो नास्ति संसारी नासंसारी च कश्चन ॥ 15.16 ॥ 141

भ्रान्तिमात्रमिदं विश्वं न किञ्चिदिति निश्चयी ।
निर्वासनः स्फूर्तिमात्रो न किञ्चिदिव शाम्यति ॥ 15.17 ॥ 142

एक एव भवाम्भोधावासीदस्ति भविष्यति ।

न ते बन्धोऽस्ति मोक्षो वा कृत्यकृत्यः सुखं चर ॥ 15.18 ॥ 143

मा सङ्कल्पविकल्पाभ्यां चित्तं क्षोभय चिन्मय ।
उपशाम्य सुखं तिष्ठ स्वात्मन्यानन्दविग्रहे ॥ 15.19 ॥ 144

त्यजैव ध्यानं सर्वत्र मा किञ्चिद् हृदि धारय ।
आत्मा त्वं मुक्त एवासि किं विमृश्य करिष्यसि ॥ 15.20 ॥ 145

## 16 षोडशं प्रकरणम् । अष्टावक्र उवाच ।

आचक्ष्व शृणु वा तात नानाशास्त्राण्यनेकशः ।
तथापि न तव स्वास्थ्यं सर्वविस्मरणाद् ऋते ॥ 16.1 ॥ 146

भोगं कर्म समाधिं वा कुरु विज्ञ तथापि ते ।
चित्तं निरस्तसर्वाशमत्यर्थं रोचयिष्यति ॥ 16.2 ॥ 147

आयासात्सकलो दुःखी नैनं जानाति कश्चन ।
अनेनैवोपदेशेन धन्यः प्राप्नोति निर्वृतिम् ॥ 16.3 ॥ 148

व्यापारे खिद्यते यस्तु निमेषोन्मेषयोरपि ।
तस्यालस्यधुरीणस्य सुखं नान्यस्य कस्यचित् ॥ 16.4 ॥ 149

इदं कृतमिदं नेति द्वन्द्वैर्मुक्तं यदा मनः ।
धर्मार्थकाममोक्षेषु निरपेक्षं तदा भवेत् ॥ 16.5 ॥ 150

विरक्तो विषयद्वेष्टा रागी विषयलोलुपः ।
ग्रहमोक्षविहीनस्तु न विरक्तो न रागवान् ॥ 16.6 ॥ 151

हेयोपादेयता तावत् संसारविटपाङ्कुरः ।
स्पृहा जीवति यावद् वै निर्विचारदशास्पदम् ॥ 16.7 ॥ 152

प्रवृत्तौ जायते रागो निर्वृत्तौ द्वेष एव हि ।
निर्द्वन्द्वो बालवद् धीमान् एवमेव व्यवस्थितः ॥ 16.8 ॥ 153

हातुमिच्छति संसारं रागी दुःखजिहासया ।
वीतरागो हि निर्दुःखस्तस्मिन्नपि न खिद्यति ॥ 16.9 ॥ 154

यस्याभिमानो मोक्षेऽपि देहेऽपि ममता तथा ।
न च ज्ञानी न वा योगी केवलं दुःखभागसौ ॥ 16.10 ॥ 155

हरो यदुपदेष्टा ते हरिः कमलजोऽपि वा ।
तथापि न तव स्वास्थ्यं सर्वविस्मरणाद् ऋते ॥ 16.11 ॥ 156


<u>17 सप्तदशं प्रकरणम्</u> । अष्टावक्र उवाच ।
तेन ज्ञानफलं प्राप्तं योगाभ्यासफलं तथा ।
तृप्तः स्वच्छेन्द्रियो नित्यमेकाकी रमते तु यः ॥ 17.1 ॥ 157

न कदाचिज्जगत्यस्मिन् तत्त्वज्ञो हन्त खिद्यति ।
यत एकेन तेनेदं पूर्णं ब्रह्माण्डमण्डलम् ॥ 17.2 ॥ 158

न जातु विषयाः केऽपि स्वारामं हर्षयन्त्यमी ।
सल्लकीपल्लवप्रीतमिवेभं निम्बपल्लवाः ॥ 17.3 ॥ 159

यस्तु भोगेषु भुक्तेषु न भवत्यधिवासिता ।
अभुक्तेषु निराकाङ्क्षी तादृशो भवदुर्लभः ॥ 17.4 ॥ 160

बुभुक्षुरिह संसारे मुमुक्षुरपि दृश्यते ।
भोगमोक्षनिराकाङ्क्षी विरलो हि महाशयः ॥ 17.5 ॥ 161

धर्मार्थकाममोक्षेषु जीविते मरणे तथा ।
कस्याप्युदारचित्तस्य हेयोपादेयता न हि ॥ 17.6 ॥ 162

वाञ्छा न विश्वविलये न द्वेषस्तस्य च स्थितौ ।
यथा जीविकया तस्माद् धन्य आस्ते यथा सुखम् ॥ 17.7 ॥ 163

कृतार्थोऽनेन ज्ञानेनेत्येवं गलितधीः कृती ।
पश्यन् शृण्वन् स्पृशन् जिघ्रन्नश्नन्नास्ते यथासुखम् ॥ 17.8 ॥ 164

शून्या दृष्टिर्वृथा चेष्टा विकलानीन्द्रियाणि च ।
न स्पृहा न विरक्तिर्वा क्षीणसंसारसागरे ॥ 17.9 ॥ 165

न जागर्ति न निद्राति नोन्मीलति न मीलति ।
अहो परदशा क्वापि वर्तते मुक्तचेतसः ॥ 17.10 ॥ 166

सर्वत्र दृश्यते स्वस्थः सर्वत्र विमलाशयः ।
समस्तवासनामुक्तो मुक्तः सर्वत्र राजते ॥ 17.11 ॥ 167

पश्यन् शृण्वन् स्पृशन् जिघ्रन्नश्नन् गृह्णन् वदन् व्रजन् ।
ईहितानीहितैर्मुक्तो मुक्त एव महाशयः ॥ 17.12 ॥ 168

न निन्दति न च स्तौति न हृष्यति न कुप्यति ।
न ददाति न गृह्णाति मुक्तः सर्वत्र नीरसः ॥ 17.13॥ 169

सानुरागां स्त्रियं दृष्ट्वा मृत्युं वा समुपस्थितम् ।
अविह्वलमनाः स्वस्थो मुक्त एव महाशयः ॥ 17.14॥ 170

सुखे दुःखे नरे नार्यां सम्पत्सु विपत्सु च ।
विशेषो नैव धीरस्य सर्वत्र समदर्शिनः ॥ 17.15॥ 171

न हिंसा नैव कारुण्यं नौद्धत्यं न च दीनता ।
नाश्चर्यं नैव च क्षोभः क्षीणसंसरणेऽनरे ॥ 17.16॥ 172

न मुक्तो विषयद्वेष्टा न वा विषयलोलुपः ।
असंसक्तमना नित्यं प्राप्ताप्राप्तमुपाश्नुते ॥ 17.17॥ 173

समाधानसमाधानहिताहितविकल्पनाः ।
शून्यचित्तो न जानाति कैवल्यमिव संस्थितः ॥ 17.18॥ 174

निर्ममो निरहङ्कारो न किञ्चिदिति निश्चितः ।
अन्तर्गलितसर्वाशः कुर्वन्नपि करोति न ॥ 17.19॥ 175

मनःप्रकाशसम्मोहस्वप्नजाड्यविवर्जितः ।
दशां कामपि सम्प्राप्तो भवेद् गलितमानसः ॥ 17.20॥ 176

## 18 अष्टादशं प्रकरणम् । अष्टावक्र उवाच ।
यस्य बोधोदये तावत् स्वप्नवद् भवति भ्रमः ।

तस्मै सुखैकरूपाय नमः शान्ताय तेजसे ॥ 18.1 ॥ 177

अर्जयित्वाखिलान् अर्थान् भोगानाप्नोति पुष्कलान् ।
न हि सर्वपरित्याजमन्तरेण सुखी भवेत् ॥ 18.2 ॥ 178

कर्तव्यदुःखमार्तण्डज्वालादग्धान्तरात्मनः ।
कुतः प्रशमपीयूषधारासारमृते सुखम् ॥ 18.3 ॥ 179

भवोऽयं भावनामात्रो न किंचित् परमर्थतः ।
नास्त्यभावः स्वभावानां भावाभावविभाविनाम् ॥ 18.4 ॥ 180

न दूरं न च संकोचाल्लब्धमेवात्मनः पदं ।
निर्विकल्पं निरायासं निर्विकारं निरंजनम् ॥ 18.5 ॥ 181

व्यामोहमात्रविरतौ स्वरूपादानमात्रतः ।
वीतशोका विराजन्ते निरावरणदृष्टयः ॥ 18.6 ॥ 182

समस्तं कल्पनामात्रमात्मा मुक्तः सनातनः ।
इति विज्ञाय धीरो हि किमभ्यस्यति बालवत् ॥ 18.7 ॥ 183

आत्मा ब्रह्मेति निश्चित्य भावाभावौ च कल्पितौ ।
निष्कामः किं विजानाति किं ब्रूते च करोति किम् ॥ 18.8 ॥ 184

अयं सोऽहमयं नाहं इति क्षीणा विकल्पना ।
सर्वमात्मेति निश्चित्य तूष्णींभूतस्य योगिनः ॥ 18.9 ॥ 185

न विक्षेपो न चैकाग्र्यं नातिबोधो न मूढता ।

न सुखं न च वा दुःखं उपशान्तस्य योगिनः ॥ 18.10 ॥ 186

स्वाराज्ये भैक्षवृत्तौ च लाभालाभे जने वने ।
निर्विकल्पस्वभावस्य न विशेषोऽस्ति योगिनः ॥ 18.11 ॥ 187

क्व धर्मः क्व च वा कामः क्व चार्थः क्व विवेकिता ।
इदं कृतमिदं नेति द्वन्द्वैर्मुक्तस्य योगिनः ॥ 18.12 ॥ 188

कृत्यं किमपि नैवास्ति न कापि हृदि रंजना ।
यथा जीवनमेवेह जीवन्मुक्तस्य योगिनः ॥ 18.13 ॥ 189

क्व मोहः क्व च वा विश्वं क्व तद्ध्यानं क्व मुक्तता ।
सर्वसंकल्पसीमायां विश्रान्तस्य महात्मनः ॥ 18.14 ॥ 190

येन विश्वमिदं दृष्टं स नास्तीति करोतु वै ।
निर्वासनः किं कुरुते पश्यन्नपि न पश्यति ॥ 18.15 ॥ 191

येन दृष्टं परं ब्रह्म सोऽहं ब्रह्मेति चिन्तयेत् ।
किं चिन्तयति निश्चिन्तो द्वितीयं यो न पश्यति ॥ 18.16 ॥ 192

दृष्टो येनात्मविक्षेपो निरोधं कुरुते त्वसौ ।
उदारस्तु न विक्षिप्तः साध्याभावात्करोति किम् ॥ 18.17 ॥ 193

धीरो लोकविपर्यस्तो वर्तमानोऽपि लोकवत् ।
नो समाधिं न विक्षेपं न लोपं स्वस्य पश्यति ॥ 18.18 ॥ 194

भावाभावविहीनो यस्तृप्तो निर्वासनो बुधः ।

नैव किंचित्कृतं तेन लोकदृष्ट्या विकुर्वता ॥ 18.19 ॥ 195

प्रवृत्तौ वा निवृत्तौ वा नैव धीरस्य दुर्ग्रहः ।
यदा यत्कर्तुमायाति तत्कृत्वा तिष्ठते सुखम् ॥ 18.20 ॥ 196

निर्वासनो निरालंबः स्वच्छन्दो मुक्तबन्धनः ।
क्षिप्तः संस्कारवातेन चेष्टते शुष्कपर्णवत् ॥ 18.21 ॥ 197

असंसारस्य तु क्वापि न हर्षो न विषादिता ।
स शीतलहृमना नित्यं विदेह इव राजये ॥ 18.22 ॥ 198

कुत्रापि न जिहासास्ति नाशो वापि न कुत्रचित् ।
आत्मारामस्य धीरस्य शीतलाच्छतरात्मनः ॥ 18.23 ॥ 199

प्रकृत्या शून्यचित्तस्य कुर्वतोऽस्य यदृच्छया ।
प्राकृतस्येव धीरस्य न मानो नावमानता ॥ 18.24 ॥ 200

कृतं देहेन कर्मेदं न मया शुद्धरूपिणा ।
इति चिन्तानुरोधी यः कुर्वन्नपि करोति न ॥ 18.25 ॥ 201

अतद्वादीव कुरुते न भवेदपि बालिशः ।
जीवन्मुक्तः सुखी श्रीमान् संसरन्नपि शोभते ॥ 18.26 ॥ 202

नाविचारसुश्रान्तो धीरो विश्रान्तिमागतः ।
न कल्पते न जाति न श्रृणोति न पश्यति ॥ 18.27 ॥ 203

असमाधेरविक्षेपान्न मुमुक्षुर्न चेतरः ।

निश्चित्य कल्पितं पश्यन् ब्रह्मैवास्ते महाशयः ॥ 18.28 ॥ 204

यस्यान्तः स्यादहंकारो न करोति करोति सः ।
निरहंकारधीरेण न किंचिदकृतं कृतम् ॥ 18.29 ॥ 205

नोद्विग्नं न च सन्तुष्टमकर्तृ स्पन्दवर्जितम् ।
निराशं गतसन्देहं चित्तं मुक्तस्य राजते ॥ 18.30 ॥ 206

निर्ध्यातुं चेष्टितुं वापि यच्चित्तं न प्रवर्तते ।
निर्निमित्तमिदं किंतु निर्ध्यायेति विचेष्टते ॥ 18.31 ॥ 207

तत्त्वं यथार्थमाकर्ण्य मन्दः प्राप्नोति मूढताम् ।
अथवा याति संकोचममूढः कोऽपि मूढवत् ॥ 18.32 ॥ 208

एकाग्रता निरोधो वा मूढैरभ्यस्यते भृशम् ।
धीराः कृत्यं न पश्यन्ति सुप्तवत्स्वपदे स्थिताः ॥ 18.33 ॥ 209

अप्रयत्नात् प्रयत्नाद् वा मूढो नाप्नोति निर्वृतिम् ।
तत्त्वनिश्चयमात्रेण प्राज्ञो भवति निर्वृतः ॥ 18.34 ॥ 210

शुद्धं बुद्धं प्रियं पूर्णं निष्प्रपंचं निरामयम् ।
आत्मानं तं न जानन्ति तत्राभ्यासपरा जनाः ॥ 18.35 ॥ 211

नाप्नोति कर्मणा मोक्षं विमूढोऽभ्यासरूपिणा ।
धन्यो विज्ञानमात्रेण मुक्तस्तिष्ठत्यविक्रियः ॥ 18.36 ॥ 212

मूढो नाप्नोति तद् ब्रह्म यतो भवितुमिच्छति ।

अनिच्छन्नपि धीरो हि परब्रह्मस्वरूपभाक् ॥ 18.37 ॥ 213

निराधारा ग्रहव्यग्रा मूढाः संसारपोषकाः ।
एतस्यानर्थमूलस्य मूलच्छेदः कृतो बुधैः ॥ 18.38 ॥ 214

न शान्तिं लभते मूढो यतः शमितुमिच्छति ।
धीरस्तत्त्वं विनिश्चित्य सर्वदा शान्तमानसः ॥ 18.39 ॥ 215

क्वात्मनो दर्शनं तस्य यद् दृष्टमवलंबते ।
धीरास्तं न पश्यन्ति पश्यन्त्यात्मानमव्ययम् ॥ 18.40 ॥ 216

क्व निरोधो विमूढस्य यो निर्बन्धं करोति वै ।
स्वारामस्यैव धीरस्य सर्वदासावकृत्रिमः ॥ 18.41 ॥ 217

भावस्य भावकः कश्चिन् न किंचिद् भावकोपरः ।
उभयाभावकः कश्चिद् एवमेव निराकुलः ॥ 18.42 ॥ 218

शुद्धमद्वयमात्मानं भावयन्ति कुबुद्धयः ।
न तु जानन्ति संमोहाद्यावज्जीवमनिर्वृताः ॥ 18.43 ॥ 219

मुमुक्षोर्बुद्धिरालंबमन्तरेण न विद्यते ।
निरालंबैव निष्कामा बुद्धिर्मुक्तस्य सर्वदा ॥ 18.44 ॥ 220

विषयद्वीपिनो वीक्ष्य चकिताः शरणार्थिनः ।
विशन्ति झटिति क्रोडं निरोधैकाग्रसिद्धये ॥ 18.45 ॥ 221

निर्वासनं हरिं दृष्ट्वा तूष्णीं विषयदन्तिनः ।

पलायन्ते न शक्तास्ते सेवन्ते कृतचाटवः ॥ 18.46 ॥ 222

न मुक्तिकारिकां धत्ते निःशङ्को युक्तमानसः ।
पश्यन् शृण्वन् स्पृशन् जिघ्रन्नश्नन्नास्ते यथासुखम् ॥ 18.47 ॥ 223

वस्तुश्रवणमात्रेण शुद्धबुद्धिर्निराकुलः ।
नैवाचारमनाचारमौदास्यं वा प्रपश्यति ॥ 18.48 ॥ 224

यदा यत्कर्तुमायाति तदा तत्कुरुते ऋजुः ।
शुभं वाप्यशुभं वापि तस्य चेष्टा हि बालवत् ॥ 18.49 ॥ 225

स्वातंत्र्यात्सुखमाप्नोति स्वातंत्र्याल्लभते परं ।
स्वातंत्र्यान्निर्वृतिं गच्छेत्स्वातंत्र्यात् परमं पदम् ॥ 18.50 ॥ 226

अकर्तृत्वमभोक्तृत्वं स्वात्मनो मन्यते यदा ।
तदा क्षीणा भवन्त्येव समस्ताश्चित्तवृत्तयः ॥ 18.51 ॥ 227

उच्छृंखलाप्यकृतिका स्थितिर्धीरस्य राजते ।
न तु सस्पृहचित्तस्य शान्तिर्मूढस्य कृत्रिमा ॥ 18.52 ॥ 228

विलसन्ति महाभोगैर्विशन्ति गिरिगह्वरान् ।
निरस्तकल्पना धीरा अबद्धा मुक्तबुद्धयः ॥ 18.53 ॥ 229

श्रोत्रियं देवतां तीर्थमङ्गनां भूपतिं प्रियं ।
दृष्ट्वा संपूज्य धीरस्य न कापि हृदि वासना ॥ 18.54 ॥ 230

भृत्यैः पुत्रैः कलत्रैश्च दौहित्रैश्चापि गोत्रजैः ।

विहस्य धिक्कृतो योगी न याति विकृतिं मनाक् ॥ 18.55॥ 231

सन्तुष्टोऽपि न सन्तुष्टः खिन्नोऽपि न च खिद्यते ।
तस्याश्चर्यदशां तां तां तादृशा एव जानते ॥ 18.56॥ 232

कर्तव्यतैव संसारो न तां पश्यन्ति सूरयः ।
शून्याकारा निराकारा निर्विकारा निरामयाः ॥ 18.57॥ 233

अकुर्वन्नपि संक्षोभाद् व्यग्रः सर्वत्र मूढधीः ।
कुर्वन्नपि तु कृत्यानि कुशलो हि निराकुलः ॥ 18.58॥ 234

सुखमास्ते सुखं शेते सुखमायाति याति च ।
सुखं वक्ति सुखं भुंक्ते व्यवहारेऽपि शान्तधीः ॥ 18.59॥ 235

स्वभावाद्यस्य नैवार्तिर्लोकवद् व्यवहारिणः ।
महाहृद इवाक्षोभ्यो गतक्लेशः स शोभते ॥ 18.60॥ 236

निवृत्तिरपि मूढस्य प्रवृत्ति रुपजायते ।
प्रवृत्तिरपि धीरस्य निवृत्तिफलभागिनी ॥ 18.61॥ 237

परिग्रहेषु वैराग्यं प्रायो मूढस्य दृश्यते ।
देहे विगलिताशास्य क्व रागः क्व विरागता ॥ 18.62॥ 238

भावनाभावनासक्ता दृष्टिर्मूढस्य सर्वदा ।
भाव्यभावनया सा तु स्वस्थस्यादृष्टिरूपिणी ॥ 18.63॥ 239

सर्वारंभेषु निष्कामो यश्चरेद् बालवन् मुनिः ।

न लेपस्तस्य शुद्धस्य क्रियमाणोऽपि कर्मणि ॥ 18.64 ॥ 240

स एव धन्य आत्मज्ञः सर्वभावेषु यः समः ।
पश्यन् शृण्वन् स्पृशन् जिघ्रन्न् अश्नन्निस्तर्षमानसः ॥ 18.65 ॥ 241

क्व संसारः क्व चाभासः क्व साध्यं क्व च साधनं ।
आकाशस्येव धीरस्य निर्विकल्पस्य सर्वदा ॥ 18.66 ॥ 242

स जयत्यर्थसंन्यासी पूर्णस्वरसविग्रहः ।
अकृत्रिमोऽनवच्छिन्ने समाधिर्यस्य वर्तते ॥ 18.67 ॥ 243

बहुनात्र किमुक्तेन ज्ञाततत्त्वो महाशयः ।
भोगमोक्षनिराकांक्षी सदा सर्वत्र नीरसः ॥ 18.68 ॥ 244

महदादि जगद्द्वैतं नाममात्रविजृंभितं ।
विहाय शुद्धबोधस्य किं कृत्यमवशिष्यते ॥ 18.69 ॥ 245

भ्रमभूतमिदं सर्वं किंचिन्नास्तीति निश्चयी ।
अलक्ष्यस्फुरणः शुद्धः स्वभावेनैव शाम्यति ॥ 18.70 ॥ 264

शुद्धस्फुरणरूपस्य दृश्यभावमपश्यतः ।
क्व विधिः क्व वैराग्यं क्व त्यागः क्व शमोऽपि वा ॥ 18.71 ॥ 247

स्फुरतोऽनन्तरूपेण प्रकृतिं च न पश्यतः ।
क्व बन्धः क्व च वा मोक्षः क्व हर्षः क्व विषादिता ॥ 18.72 ॥ 248

बुद्धिपर्यन्तसंसारे मायामात्रं विवर्तते ।

निर्ममो निरहंकारो निष्कामः शोभते बुधः ॥ 18.73॥ 249

अक्षयं गतसन्तापमात्मानं पश्यतो मुनेः ।
क्व विद्या च क्व वा विश्वं क्व देहोऽहं ममेति वा ॥ 18.74॥ 250

निरोधादीनि कर्माणि जहाति जडधीर्यदि ।
मनोरथान् प्रलापांश्च कर्तुमाप्नोत्यतत्क्षणात् ॥ 18.75॥ 251

मन्दः श्रुत्वापि तद्वस्तु न जहाति विमूढतां ।
निर्विकल्पो बहिर्यत्नादन्तर्विषयलालसः ॥ 18.76॥ 252

ज्ञानाद् गलितकर्मा यो लोकदृष्ट्यापि कर्मकृत् ।
नाप्नोत्यवसरं कर्म वक्तुमेव न किंचन ॥ 18.77॥ 253

क्व तमः क्व प्रकाशो वा हानं क्व च न किंचन ।
निर्विकारस्य धीरस्य निरातंकस्य सर्वदा ॥ 18.78॥ 254

क्व धैर्यं क्व विवेकित्वं क्व निरातंकतापि वा ।
अनिर्वाच्यस्वभावस्य निःस्वभावस्य योगिनः ॥ 18.79॥ 255

न स्वर्गो नैव नरको जीवन्मुक्तिर्न चैव हि ।
बहुनात्र किमुक्तेन योगदृष्ट्या न किंचन ॥ 18.80॥ 256

नैव प्रार्थयते लाभं नालाभेनानुशोचति ।
धीरस्य शीतलं चित्तममृतेनैव पूरितम् ॥ 18.81॥ 257

न शान्तं स्तौति निष्कामो न दुष्टमपि निन्दति ।

समदुःखसुखस्तृप्तः किंचित् कृत्यं न पश्यति ॥ 18.82॥ 258

धीरो न द्वेष्टि संसारमात्मानं न दिदृक्षति ।
हर्षामर्षविनिर्मुक्तो न मृतो न च जीवति ॥ 18.83॥ 259

निःस्नेहः पुत्रदारादौ निष्कामो विषयेषु च ।
निश्चिन्तः स्वशरीरेऽपि निराशः शोभते बुधः ॥ 18.84॥ 260

तुष्टिः सर्वत्र धीरस्य यथापतितवर्तिनः ।
स्वच्छन्दं चरतो देशान् यत्रस्तमितशायिनः ॥ 18.85॥ 261

पततूदेतु वा देहो नास्य चिन्ता महात्मनः ।
स्वभावभूमिविश्रान्तिविस्मृताशेषसंसृतेः ॥ 18.86॥ 262

अकिंचनः कामचारो निर्द्वन्द्वश्छिन्नसंशयः ।
असक्तः सर्वभावेषु केवलो रमते बुधः ॥ 18.87॥ 263

निर्ममः शोभते धीरः समलोष्टाश्मकांचनः ।
सुभिन्नहृदयग्रन्थिर्विनिर्धूतरजस्तमः ॥ 18.88॥ 264

सर्वत्रानवधानस्य न किंचिद् वासना हृदि ।
मुक्तात्मनो वितृप्तस्य तुलना केन जायते ॥ 18.89॥ 265

जानन्नपि न जानाति पश्यन्नपि न पश्यति ।
ब्रुवन्न् अपि न च ब्रूते कोऽन्यो निर्वासनादृते ॥ 18.90॥ 266

भिक्षुर्वा भूपतिर्वापि यो निष्कामः स शोभते ।

भावेषु गलिता यस्य शोभनाशोभना मतिः ॥ 18.91 ॥ 267

क्व स्वाच्छन्द्यं क्व संकोचः क्व वा तत्त्वविनिश्चयः ।
निर्व्याजार्जवभूतस्य चरितार्थस्य योगिनः ॥ 18.92 ॥ 268

आत्मविश्रान्तितृप्तेन निराशेन गतार्तिना ।
अन्तर्यदनुभूयेत तत् कथं कस्य कथ्यते ॥ 18.93 ॥ 269

सुप्तोऽपि न सुषुप्तौ च स्वप्नेऽपि शयितो न च ।
जागरेऽपि न जागर्ति धीरस्तृप्तः पदे पदे ॥ 18.94 ॥ 270

ज्ञः सचिन्तोऽपि निश्चिन्तः सेन्द्रियोऽपि निरिन्द्रियः ।
सुबुद्धिरपि निर्बुद्धिः साहंकारोऽनहंकृतिः ॥ 18.95 ॥ 271

न सुखी न च वा दुःखी न विरक्तो न संगवान् ।
न मुमुक्षुर्न वा मुक्ता न किंचिन्न च किंचन ॥ 18.96 ॥ 272

विक्षेपेऽपि न विक्षिप्तः समाधौ न समाधिमान् ।
जाड्येऽपि न जडो धन्यः पाण्डित्येऽपि न पण्डितः ॥ 18.97 ॥ 273

मुक्तो यथास्थितिस्वस्थः कृतकर्तव्यनिर्वृतः ।
समः सर्वत्र वैतृष्ण्यान्न स्मरत्यकृतं कृतम् ॥ 18.98 ॥ 274

न प्रीयते वन्द्यमानो निन्द्यमानो न कुप्यति ।
नैवोद्विजति मरणे जीवने नाभिनन्दति ॥ 18.99 ॥ 275

न धावति जनाकीर्णं नारण्यमुपशान्तधीः ।
यथातथा यत्रतत्र सम एवावतिष्ठते ॥ 18.100 ॥ 276


<u>19 नवदशं प्रकरणम्</u> । <u>जनक उवाच</u> ।
तत्त्वविज्ञानसन्दंशमादाय हृदयोदरात् ।
नानाविधपरामर्शशल्योद्धारः कृतो मया ॥ 19.1 ॥ 277


क्व धर्मः क्व च वा कामः क्वार्थः क्व विवेकिता ।
क्व द्वैतं क्व च वाऽद्वैतं स्वमहिम्नि स्थितस्य मे ॥ 19.2 ॥ 278


क्व भूतं क्व भविष्यद् वा वर्तमानमपि क्व वा ।
क्व देशः क्व च वा नित्यं स्वमहिम्नि स्थितस्य मे ॥ 19.3 ॥ 279


क्व चात्मा क्व च वानात्मा क्व शुभं क्वाशुभं यथा ।
क्व चिन्ता क्व च वाचिन्ता स्वमहिम्नि स्थितस्य मे ॥ 19.4 ॥ 280


क्व स्वप्नः क्व सुषुप्तिर्वा क्व च जागरणं तथा ।
क्व तुरीयं भयं वापि स्वमहिम्नि स्थितस्य मे ॥ 19.5 ॥ 281


क्व दूरं क्व समीपं वा बाह्यं क्वाभ्यन्तरं क्व वा ।
क्व स्थूलं क्व च वा सूक्ष्मं स्वमहिम्नि स्थितस्य मे ॥ 19.6 ॥ 282


क्व मृत्युर्जीवितं वा क्व लोकाः क्वास्य क्व लौकिकम् ।
क्व लयः क्व समाधिर्वा स्वमहिम्नि स्थितस्य मे ॥ 19.7 ॥ 283

अलं त्रिवर्गकथया योगस्य कथयाप्यलम् ।
अलं विज्ञानकथया विश्रान्तस्य मम आत्मनि ॥ 19.8 ॥ 284


20 विंशतितमं प्रकरणम् । जनक उवाच ।
क्व भूतानि क्व देहो वा क्वेन्द्रियाणि क्व वा मनः ।
क्व शून्यं क्व च नैराश्यं मत्स्वरूपे निरञ्जने ॥ 20.1 ॥ 285

क्व शास्त्रं क्वात्मविज्ञानं क्व वा निर्विषयं मनः ।
क्व तृप्तिः क्व वितृष्णत्वं गतद्वन्द्वस्य मे सदा ॥ 20.2 ॥ 286

क्व विद्या क्व च वाविद्या क्वाहं क्वेदं मम क्व वा ।
क्व बन्धः क्व च वा मोक्षः स्वरूपस्य क्व रूपिता ॥ 20.3 ॥ 287

क्व प्रारब्धानि कर्माणि जीवन्मुक्तिरपि क्व वा ।
क्व तद् विदेहकैवल्यं निर्विशेषस्य सर्वदा ॥ 20.4 ॥ 288

क्व कर्ता क्व च वा भोक्ता निष्क्रियं स्फुरणं क्व वा ।
क्वापरोक्षं फलं वा क्व निःस्वभावस्य मे सदा ॥ 20.5 ॥ 289

क्व लोकं क्व मुमुक्षुर्वा क्व योगी ज्ञानवान् क्व वा ।
क्व बद्धः क्व च वा मुक्तः स्वस्वरूपेऽहमद्वये ॥ 20.6 ॥ 290

क्व सृष्टिः क्व च संहारः क्व साध्यं क्व च साधनं ।
क्व साधकः क्व सिद्धिर्वा स्वस्वरूपेऽहमद्वये ॥ 20.7 ॥ 291

क्व प्रमाता प्रमाणं वा क्व प्रमेयं क्व च प्रमा ।

क किञ्चित् क न किञ्चिद्धा सर्वदा विमलस्य मे ॥ 20.8 ॥ 292

क विक्षेपः क चैकाग्र्यं क निर्बोधः क मूढता ।
क हर्षः क विषादो वा सर्वदा निष्क्रियस्य मे ॥ 20.9 ॥ 293

क चैष व्यवहारो वा क च सा परमार्थता ।
क सुखं क च वा दुखं निर्विमर्शस्य मे सदा ॥ 20.10 ॥ 294

क माया क च संसारः क प्रीतिर्विरतिः क वा ।
क जीवः क च तद् ब्रह्म सर्वदा विमलस्य मे ॥ 20.11 ॥ 295

क प्रवृत्तिर्निवृत्तिर्वा क मुक्तिः क च बन्धनम् ।
कूटस्थनिर्विभागस्य स्वस्थस्य मम सर्वदा ॥ 20.12 ॥ 296

क्कोपदेशः क वा शास्त्रं क शिष्यः क च वा गुरुः ।
क चास्ति पुरुषार्थो वा निरुपाधेः शिवस्य मे ॥ 20.13 ॥ 297

क चास्ति क च वा नास्ति कास्ति चैकं क च द्वयम् ।
बहुनात्र किमुक्तेन किञ्चिन्नोत्तिष्ठते मम ॥ 20.14 ॥ 298

॥ ॐ तत्सत् ॥

# Sanskrit Grammar

Sandhis separated word by word पदच्छेद (प०),

Verses in prose order अन्वय (अ०), and with विभक्ति Cases.

Abbreviations
Nouns
    **m** masculine, **f** feminine, **n** neuter; **V** vocative
    **1/1** = vibhakti case from 1 to 7/number 1 to 3

Indeclinables (uninflected nouns or verbs) **0**
In Sanskrit the **adverbs** are mostly uninflected.

Verbs
    **iii/1** = person i to iii / number 1 to 3

    **PPP** = Past Participle Passive = क्त

    **PPA** = Past Participle Active = क्तवत्

    **PrPA** = PresentParticiple Active = शतृ / शानच्

    **PoPP** = PotentialParticiple Passive = य, तव्य, अनीयर्
    (gerund)

    तुमुन् = infinitive, in the sense of "to do"

Anusvara and Makara have been kept as they are in Padacheda, to avoid over work. E.g. इदं should be written as इदम् in Padacheda.

Sanskrit Literature frequently omits the verb – "is". The words भवति, अस्ति etc. are implicit.

E.g. तत्परा योनिमुक्ताः ॥ १.७ = तत्परा योनिमुक्ताः भवन्ति ॥

Since Sanskrit is an inflectional language, the **spelling of the same word** changes as per context or usage. Hence words can be **placed anywhere** in a sentence, as in poetic use, without change in meaning. The matrix shows how.

## Verb inflections in Sanskrit – a sample chart

| 982 गम् गतौ – to go, also in the sense of attainment | | | |
|---|---|---|---|
| Present Tense Active voice लट् कर्तरि प्रयोगः | | | |
| Person/no | singular | dual | plural |
| Third | गच्छति [iii/1] | गच्छतः [iii/2] | गच्छन्ति [iii/3] |
| Second | गच्छसि [ii/1] | गच्छथः [ii/2] | गच्छथ [ii/3] |
| First | गच्छामि [i/1] | गच्छावः [i/2] | गच्छामः [i/3] |

## Noun declensions in Sanskrit – a sample chart

| Masculine stem, vowel अ ending | | | |
|---|---|---|---|
| (र्–आ–म्–अ) राम[m] Lord's name | | | |
| | singular[1] | dual[2] | plural[3] |
| 1 Doer | रामः [1/1] | रामौ [1/2] | रामाः [1/3] |
| 2 Object | रामम् [2/1] | रामौ [2/2] | रामान् [2/3] |
| 3 by | रामेण [3/1] | रामाभ्याम् [3/2] | रामैः [3/3] |
| 4 for | रामाय [4/1] | रामाभ्याम् [4/2] | रामेभ्यः [4/3] |
| 5 from | रामात् [5/1] | रामाभ्याम् [5/2] | रामेभ्यः [5/3] |
| 6 of | रामस्य [6/1] | रामयोः [6/2] | रामाणाम् [6/3] |
| 7 in | रामे [7/1] | रामयोः [7/2] | रामेषु [7/3] |
| Vocative | हे राम [V/1] | हे रामौ [V/2] | हे रामाः [V/3] |

| Masculine stem, consonant त् ending |||| 
|---|---|---|---|
| मरुत्[m] Wind, Breeze, Air |||| 
|  | singular[1] | dual [2] | plural [3] |
| 1 Doer | मरुत् [1/1] | मरुतौ [1/2] | मरुतः [1/3] |
| 2 Object | मरुतम् [2/1] | मरुतौ [2/2] | मरुतः [2/3] |
| 3 by | मरुता [3/1] | मरुद्भ्याम् [3/2] | मरुद्भिः [3/3] |
| 4 for | मरुते [4/1] | मरुद्भ्याम् [4/2] | मरुद्भ्यः [4/3] |
| 5 from | मरुतः [5/1] | मरुद्भ्याम् [5/2] | मरुद्भ्यः [5/3] |
| 6 of | मरुतः [6/1] | मरुतोः [6/2] | मरुताम् [6/3] |
| 7 in | मरुति [7/1] | मरुतोः [7/2] | मरुत्सु [7/3] |
| Vocative | हे मरुत् [V/1] | हे मरुतौ [V/2] | हे मरुतः [V/3] |

## Moods and Tenses in Sanskrit

| 1 | लट् | Present Tense |
|---|---|---|
| 2 | लुङ् | Aorist Past Tense, *before from now onwards* |
| 3 | लङ् | Imperfect Past Tense – *before from yesterday onwards* |
| 4 | लिट् | Perfect Past Tense – *distant unseen past* |
| 5 | लृट् | Simple Future Tense – *now onwards* |
| 6 | लुट् | Periphrastic Future Tense – *tomorrow onwards* |
| 7 | लृङ् | Conditional Mood - *if/then in past or future* |
| 8 | लोट् | Imperative Mood – *request* |
| 9 | विधि– | Potential Mood – *order* विधिलिङ् (also |

| | लिङ् | known as Optative Mood) |
|---|---|---|
| 10 | आशीर्-लिङ् | Benedictive Mood – *blessing* आशीर्लिङ् (also used in the sense of a curse) |

# Conjugation process of Verb

वदन्ति = they say, they describe.
1st conjugation Root, Parasmaipadi.
1009 √ वदँ व्यक्तायां वाचि । to tell, relate, describe.

1.3.1 भूवादयो धातवः । वदँ = वदुअँ ।

1.3.2 उपदेशेऽजनुनासिक इत् । 1.3.9 तस्य लोपः । वदु ।

3.4.69 लः कर्मणि च भावे चाकर्मकेभ्यः । वदु ।

3.2.123 वर्तमाने लट् । 3.4.77 लस्य । वदु + लँट् ।

1.3.3 हलन्त्यम् । 1.3.9 तस्य लोपः । वदु+लँ ।

1.3.2 उपदेशेऽजनुनासिक इत् । 1.3.9तस्य लोपः । वदु+ल् ।

3.4.78 तिप्तस्झिसिप्थस्थमिब्वस्मस् तातांझथासाथांध्वमिड्वहिमहिङ् ।

1.4.199 लः परस्मैपदम् । choose Parasmaipada affix.

वदु+झि । we are conjugating third person

1.4.101 तिङस्त्रीणि त्रीणि प्रथममध्यमोत्तमाः ।

1.4.102 तान्येकवचनद्विवचनबहुवचनान्येकशः । वदु+झि । plural

1.4.108 शेषे प्रथमः । वदु+झि । this is called "प्रथमः" i.e. the **first and most** used in language, third person.

3.4.113 तिङ्शित्सार्वधातुकम् । वदु+झि ।

3.1.68 कर्त्तरि शप् । वद्+शप्+झि ।

3.4.113 तिङ्शित्सार्वधातुकम् । वद्+शप्+झि ।

7.1.3 झोऽन्तः । वद्+शप्+ अन्ति ।

1.3.3 हलन्त्यम्। 1.3.8लशक्वतद्धिते। 1.3.9तस्य लोपः।वद्+अ+अन्ति ।

6.1.97 अतो गुणे । वद्+अन्ति । sandhi drops the अकारः ।

8.3.24 नश्चापदान्तस्य झलि । वद् + अंति । Anusvara appears

8.4.58 अनुस्वारस्य ययि परसवर्णः । वद् + अन्ति ।

Anusvara again changes to नकारः ।

वद् + अन्ति = वदन्ति $^{iii/3\ लट्}$ । iii = 3$^{rd}$ person, 3 = plural.
Third person plural, Present Tense.

# Declension process of Noun

ब्रह्म = Brahma. The Lord. Highest Intelligence.

Stem Brahman ब्रह्मन् n → ब्रह्म neuter Nominative $^{1/1}$
The Great Lord. The Invisible presence.

1.2.45 अर्थवद्धातुरप्रत्ययः प्रातिपदिकम् । ब्रह्मन्

1.2.46 कृत्तद्धितसमासाश्च । 3.1.1 प्रत्ययः । 3.1.2 परश्च ।

4.1.1 ङ्याप्प्रातिपदिकात् । 4.1.2 स्वौजस्-मौट्छष्टाभ्याम्भिस्ङेभ्याम्यस्ङसिभ्याम्यस्ङसोसाम्ङ्योस्सुप् ।

1.4.104 विभक्तिश्च । 1.4.103 सुपः = use one of these vibhakti suffix. ब्रह्मन् + सुँ ।

1.4.22 द्व्येकयोर्द्विवचनैकवचने = singular number taken.
ब्रह्मन् + सुँ ।

7.1.23 स्वमोर्नपुंसकात् । 2.4.13 यस्मात्प्रत्ययविधिस्तदादि प्रत्ययेऽङ्गम् ।
6.4.1 अङ्गस्य । 1st and 2nd case Vibhakti drops for neuter stem. ब्रह्मन् ।

1.4.17 स्वादिष्वसर्वनामस्थाने । The word gets पदसंज्ञा ।
ब्रह्मन् ।

8.2.7 न लोपः प्रातिपदिकान्तस्य । Final नकार drops.

ब्रह्म $^{n1/1}$ । *Neuter. First case nominative singular.* **Brahma.**
The Highest. The Supreme. Shiva. Purusha. Tao.
The Beautiful, The Love, The Infinite, The Divine.
Any name is **Him.**
All directions point to **It**. Every form is **She.**

# References

Sri Sri Ravi Shankar - Ashtavakra Gita English Commentary (Live) - 1st – 1991
https://www.amazon.in/Ashtavakra-Gita-Sri-Ravi-Shankar/dp/9380592833

Sri Sri Ravi Shankar - Ashtavakra Gita Hindi Commentary (Live) - 1st – 2010
https://garudabooks.com/ashtavakra-gita-hindi

Radhakamal Mukerjee – AstavakraGita (The Song of the Self Supreme) – 1st – 1971 (7th Reprint 2014) – Motilal Banarsidass, Delhi.

Swami Nityaswarupananda – Ashtavakra Samhita – 1st – 1940 – Advaita Ashrama, Almora, Himalayas.

Babu Jalim Singh – अष्टावक्र गीता – 1st – 1971 – Tejkumar Book Depot, Lucknow.

Ashwini Kumar Aggarwal
    – Dhatupatha of Panini – 2nd – 2017 –
    – Sanskrit Sandhi Handbook – 1st – 2019 –
    – Sanskrit Nouns Sabda Manjari – 1st – 2019 –
Devotees of Sri Sri Ravi Shankar Ashram, Punjab.

https://www.ashtangayoga.info/philosophy/sanskrit-and-devanagari/transliteration-tool/
https://www.learnsanskrit.cc/   http://sanskrit.segal.net.br/
https://sa.wikisource.org/wiki/%E0%A4%85%E0%A4%B7%E0%A5%8D%E0%A4%9F%E0%A4%BE%E0%A4%B5%E0%A4%95%E0%A5%8D%E0%A4%B0%E0%A4%97%E0%A5%80%E0%A4%A4%E0%A4%BE
https://www.artofliving.org/us-en/wisdom/ashtavakra-gita

# Epilogue

Life is Precious. Live every moment in Gratefulness, Kindness, Cheerfulness, Joy.

IT IS NOT EASY WITHOUT A MASTER.

सर्वे भवन्तु सुखिनः । सर्वे सन्तु निरामयाः ।
सर्वे भद्राणि पश्यन्तु । मा कश्चिद् दुःख भाग्भवेत् ॥
ॐ शान्तिः शान्तिः शान्तिः ॥

When faith has blossomed in life,
Every step is led by the Divine.
Sri Sri Ravi Shankar

**Om Namah Shivaya**

जय गुरुदेव

www.ingramcontent.com/pod-product-compliance
Lightning Source LLC
LaVergne TN
LVHW091539070526
838199LV00002B/127